ALL POINTS GUIDE

LIVE GLOBALLY, EARN REMOTELY & PAY LESS TAX

A SPECIAL REPORT FOR U.S. TAXPAYERS

ALL POINTS GUIDE

LIVE GLOBALLY, EARN REMOTELY & PAY LESS TAX

A SPECIAL REPORT FOR U.S. TAXPAYERS

Jason S. Guetzkow, Esq.

A Dime Group LLC Publication

AllPointsGuide Live Globally, Earn Remotely and Pay Less Tax: A Special Report for U.S. Taxpayers / Jason S. Guetzkow
ISBN: 979-8-9878227-2-2

THE AUTHOR

Jason S. Guetzkow, Esq., is a graduate of UC Berkeley and the New York University School of Law. As a practicing attorney in the United States, he has been advising private clients about tax, business, probate, estate planning, long-term care and real estate issues for more than 25 years. Since 2015, he has served as the trustee of commercial and residential real estate with a total value of over $200 million US dollars.

DEDICATION

This book is dedicated to James, Charolette, Joshua, Sandra, Noam and Eyal for all their help and support and to Gabriella for continuing to inspire us all with her resilience, resolve and bravery.

Thanks to Steve, Michelle, Michael and Melissa for helping to make Washington, D.C. feel like home.

And an extra special dose of thanks to Charolette for patiently and thoroughly editing this book prior to publication.

IMPORTANT DISCLAIMERS

This book is not meant to comprise legal, medical, financial or tax advice specifically meant for your unique needs or concerns, and its contents are only intended to point out general principles of life in foreign countries for informational purposes.

Furthermore, your purchase or reading of this book does not establish an attorney/client relationship or any other kind of fiduciary relationship between you and the author(s) and/or publisher(s) of this book.

We recommend that you confirm any information or conclusions in this book that you believe are relevant to you with one or more competent legal, medical, financial, insurance, construction, engineering and/or tax professionals in the appropriate and applicable jurisdictions and obtain their advice or counsel before taking any actions on your own, especially if those actions are related to the laws, rules, medical matters, financial matters, insurance matters and/or tax matters the United States, and/or any other country or countries.

Finally, any statement in this book that is true at the time of this writing may no longer be true at the time that you are reading this so you should research the current status of the topics contained in this book before acting or refraining from acting based on the information contained in this book.

CONTENTS

1. THE POWER OF KNOWLEDGE

This book is mainly focused on people that are currently working remotely or at least have the option of working remotely if they want it. There is still plenty of useful material for retirees, however.

Probably most people have the option of working remotely even if they don't realize it, and in Chapter 9 we discuss a wide range of possible ways to earn money by working remotely.

Some people may want to come out of retirement after reading this book because the ability to make more money doing something enjoyable while living in a different country and paying less tax on what you make is truly compelling.

THE BIG QUESTION

"If the foreign country I am living in does not tax my income, does that mean I don't have to pay any income tax at all?"

The answer to this is probably, "No, you aren't free from all income tax obligations."

Federal Income Tax Obligations

As long as you are considered a taxpayer by the United States, then you will have to continue paying tax to the United States Treasury (through its agency, the Internal Revenue Service or IRS).

State Income Tax Obligations

In addition to federal income tax obligations, you might also have state income tax obligations. To learn more about your state income tax obligations and the possibility of relocating to a state with no income tax, see the section on "State Income Tax" in Chapter 14.

The Good News

The good news is that you might have to pay less tax to the IRS if you meet certain requirements that we discuss in detail in Chapter 14.

The beautiful thing is that it doesn't matter where the source of your income is located. It could be coming from the U.S. or anywhere else in the world. As long as *you* are living abroad, then you might be eligible for a huge tax break in the form of the Foreign Earned Income Exclusion. If you are eligible for the Foreign Earned Income Exclusion, then you might also be eligible for either the Foreign Housing Deduction or the Foreign Housing Exclusion, discussed in detail in Chapter 14.

THE CONCEPT OF THIS BOOK

The idea of this book is that you should try to avoid being taxed by foreign countries and seek instead to be taxed by the U.S. at the federal level. To do this, you can find out what countries are less likely to tax you on your income, especially income that comes from a source located outside that country.

Provided that you continue to be eligible for the tax savings discussed in Chapter 14, you can save a significant amount of money year after year on your U.S. taxes. This is true even if the source of that money, such as your employer and/or customers, is located *inside* the United States.

At the same time, paying into the U.S. Treasury means that you can potentially increase your future Social Security benefits. If you were paying income taxes to a foreign country, then you would be missing out on that advantage.

THE NEED FOR EXPERT ADVICE

This book is an excellent starting point in becoming better informed about healthcare, tax, legal and financial information. It is not, however, the end point. It is vital that you gather around yourself expert healthcare, legal, financial and tax expertise in both the country or countries that you are living in and in your country of origin. Moreover, we recommend that you find people that have expertise in health, financial, legal and tax issues that have expertise in the SPECIALIZED NEEDS OF RETIREES, EXPATS AND/OR DIGITAL NOMADS.

For instance, if your country of origin is the United States, rather than seeking out just any C.P.A. in the U.S. to help you file your U.S. taxes, we recommend that you find a C.P.A. in the U.S. that specializes in helping retirees, expats and/or digital nomads living in foreign countries.

Two Sets of Professionals

Please also note that you may need help from TWO SETS OF PROFESSIONALS FOR EACH NEED: one in the country in which you are living and one in your country of origin. For instance, if you are living in Mexico, you might discover that you want to hire an estate planning attorney in the United States to prepare U.S. estate planning documents for use in the U.S. and also hire an attorney in Mexico called a *notario* to prepare estate planning documents for use in Mexico. As another example, you might decide you need to hire an accountant in the United States as well as an accountant in Thailand to make sure that you are fulfilling your tax reporting and/or payment obligations for both countries.

We will be discussing all these issues in greater depth throughout this book.

THE VALUE OF ALL POINTS GUIDE LIVE GLOBALLY, EARN REMOTELY & PAY LESS TAX

This book offers tremendous value to the reader. It can help people stay safe, secure and healthy: All of which have a value that is beyond price. It can also save people, potentially, hundreds of thousands of U.S. dollars over the course of their lifetimes by helping them make the smartest financial and tax-related decisions possible both individually and, potentially, as a couple.

The Most Vital Pieces of Information in This Book

In Chapter 13, we provide a detailed analysis of the potential advantages and disadvantages of renting vs. buying. Making the right choice could save you hundreds of thousands of U.S. dollars.

If you are a U.S. taxpayer who is mostly or 100% retired and drawing on Social Security, pensions and retirement accounts, then the discussion of the Federal Tax Credit (FTC) in Chapter 14 could potentially save your family tens of thousands of dollars each year that you are living outside the U.S.

Alternatively, if you are a U.S. taxpayer who will be making most of your money working remotely from outside the U.S., then the discussion of Foreign Earned Income Exclusion (FEIE) also in Chapter 14 could potentially save you, as an individual or as a couple, tens of thousands of U.S. dollars each year that you are living outside the U.S.

In conclusion, we are confident that whether you consider yourself to be a retiree, an expat, a digital nomad or just someone who likes to spend time in Country X, this book will prove to be an invaluable resource.

THE MEANING OF "COUNTRY X"

"Country X" is whatever country you are thinking about living in. Because we don't know the identity of the country you are thinking about living in, we refer to it generically as "Country X." Unless the country you are thinking about is named and described in this book, we can only speak about countries in generalities, and you will need to do further research about the specific country or countries that you plan to visit, live in or move to.

For more resources and additional information to help you start an exciting new chapter in your life, please visit our website at www.AllPointsGuide.com.

2. HOW TO SELECT AN OPTIMAL COUNTRY

WHEN DECIDING IF YOU WANT TO LIVE in a country, there are four major aspects of the nation to consider.

Here are the factors to consider:

1. Its **income tax** policies
2. The **quality of life** that the country offers
3. The **cost of living** in that country
4. Your **ability to gain access** to the country

If you find a country that overlaps on the positive sides of these categories (its tax laws are advantageous for you, the quality of life is good, the cost of living is relatively low and it will allow you to stay there for the right amount of time), then you might be homing in on a "Goldilocks" country that is just right for you. People tend to focus on only one or two of these categories only to be heartbroken when they find out that the country that they like is too expensive or won't let them live there.

Of course, you might not be sensitive to one of these factors. For instance, you might have plenty of money and so you are not as sensitive to the cost of living in a given country. That's fine. You can ignore that feature of the country and focus on the other three factors.

In another scenario, you might only plan to stay in a country for a 3-month period once or twice per year. You can live in Country X and then bounce to another country for another, say, 3-month period. In those instances, the fact that a long-term residency visa in Country X is hard to come by might be irrelevant to you.

You might, therefore, not need a country that meshes on all four of the major aspects listed above. But at least you have a general framework for making your decisions, one that allows you to tailor it for your specific needs.

Next, we are going to examine each one of these aspects in greater detail and provide some lists that will help you to identify the country or countries that might be your next Country X.

RIGHT COUNTRIES: A TAX PERSPECTIVE

Essentially, there are three different kinds of countries when it comes to how they tax the income of foreigners, and we will be discussing them in the next three chapters in greater detail. You will want to pay close attention to the next three chapters because, if you choose the wrong country from a tax perspective, it could cost you tens of thousands of dollars per year in otherwise avoidable taxes.

Three Different Categories of Countries

In the next three chapters, we are going to examine three categories of countries that, from a tax perspective, tend to not tax foreign income.

Here are the three categories that you want Country X to fall into starting with the most favorable:

Category 1: Those countries that do not tax income at all comprise this first category.

Category 2: Those countries that do not tax foreign income at all comprise this second category.

Category 3: Those countries that generally do not tax foreign income of nonresidents comprise this third category.

You may want to prioritize countries that are in the first two categories, therefore, if you are especially sensitive to tax concerns, and be extra careful when living in Category 3 countries to minimize your risks of having your foreign income taxed.

By living in a category 1 or category 2 country, you do not need to worry about becoming a resident of the country and can, therefore, live in such a country for as long as you like without having your foreign income taxed.

By the way, we are not saying that your foreign income will not be taxed by *any* country. As a U.S. citizen or resident, you will still be obligated to pay *U.S.* taxes. There may be a way, however, to minimize your U.S. taxes while living abroad, and that will be discussed in detail in Chapter 14.

Note that the mere fact that a country does not tax any income at all (or the fact that a country does not tax any *foreign* income at all) does not necessarily make it a favorable country from an overall tax perspective. This is because such countries may have other kinds of tax requirements to make up for their loss of income tax as a revenue source. Some of these other tax requirements might include such items as consumption taxes (as in VAT or sales tax), import tariffs, property taxes, social security contributions, transfer taxes, acquisition taxes, stamp taxes, gift taxes, estate taxes, net wealth taxes, net worth taxes, exit taxes and possibly even (though unlikely) pet, church and poll taxes. Make sure that you investigate each country thoroughly to find out what its taxation policies are and if any of those tax policies might disqualify a country as an attractive place to live from your viewpoint.

Also, a country might have no income tax but be so expensive to live in that you would actually be better off in a country that has income tax but is a much cheaper place in which to live.

We are now going to go through each of the three categories in the next three chapters.

☆ ☆ ☆ ☆ ☆

For more resources and additional information to help you start an exciting new chapter in your life, please visit our website at www.AllPointsGuide.com.

3. COUNTRIES WITH NO INCOME TAX

SOME COUNTRIES have no income tax whatsoever. You could say that these countries are the gold medalists when it comes to their tax laws. Note that the mere fact that a country does not tax any income at all (or even the fact that a country does not tax any foreign income at all) does not necessarily make it a favorable country from an overall tax perspective.

To understand a country's overall tax policies, you have to determine if there are other kinds of tax requirements to make up for their loss of income tax as a revenue source. Some of these other tax requirements might include such items as consumption taxes (as in VAT or sales tax), import tariffs, property taxes, social security contributions, transfer taxes, acquisition taxes, stamp taxes, gift taxes, estate taxes, net wealth taxes, net worth taxes, exit taxes and possibly even (though unlikely) pet, church and poll taxes. Make sure that you investigate each country thoroughly to find out if a specific country's overall tax policies might undercut the advantage of living in a country with no income tax.

Also, a country in this category might have no income tax but be so expensive to live in that you would be better off in a country that has income tax but is a much cheaper place in which to live.

If You Are Not Taxed on Foreign Income by Country X

As we mentioned in Chapter 1 as an answer to the Big Question, don't forget that just because you are not paying income tax in Country X, it does not necessarily mean that you do not have to pay any income tax anywhere in the world at all. You may **still be obligated to pay U.S. income taxes**, provided you are viewed as a taxpayer by the U.S.

The good news is that, if you are not paying income tax to Country X, then you might only have to pay U.S. income tax on that "foreign income" (which might have a source inside the U.S. or anywhere else in the world).

The even better news is that paying U.S. income tax on that income, regardless of the source of that income, *while living abroad* might make you eligible to benefit from the Foreign Earned Income Exclusion (FEIE). If you are eligible for the FEIE, then you might be eligible for either the Foreign Housing Deduction or the Foreign Housing Exclusion. See Chapter 14 for more information.

Again, it doesn't matter if your foreign income has a U.S. source to be eligible for U.S. tax savings. The key is that you are earning it while living abroad.

COUNTRIES WITH NO INCOME TAX
(in alphabetical order)

1. The Bahamas
2. Bermuda
3. The British Virgin Islands
4. Brunei
5. Cayman Islands
6. Kuwait
7. The Maldives
8. Monaco
9. Nauru
10. Norfolk Island
11. Oman
12. Pitcairn
13. Qatar
14. Saint Barthélemy
15. Saint Kitts and Nevis
16. Somalia
17. Turks and Caicos
18. The United Arab Emirates
19. Vanuatu
20. Vatican City State
21. Wallis and Futuna
22. Western Sahara

The prospect of not paying income tax is certainly appealing. A drawback to many of the countries listed above, however, is that they are either very expensive places to live or they may present as very unattractive places to live for one or more of many reasons such as the country's political stability and/or the level of freedom and tolerance prevalent in the country's society. You might, however, be able to find some sweet spots on the list that work for you.

Considering that some of the 22 countries listed above might not be appealing, we have eliminated 7 of them from our list. Listed below are the 15 most favorable countries that do not have an income tax, starting with the country that we view as the most favorable (paying no attention to how expensive these countries might be):

1: The Bahamas

2: Saint Kitts and Nevis

3: Turks and Caicos

4: Saint Barthélemy

5: Wallis and Futuna

6: Vanuatu

7: Bahrain

8: The British Virgin Islands

9: Cayman Islands

10: Norfolk Island

11: Pitcairn

12: The United Arab Emirates

13: Nauru

14: Monaco

15: The Maldives

We should probably point out that, unless you are a cardinal of the Catholic Church, living at the Vatican is unlikely to be an option.

☆ ☆ ☆ ☆ ☆

For more resources and additional information to help you start an exciting new chapter in your life, please visit our website at www.AllPointsGuide.com.

4. COUNTRIES WITH NO TAX ON FOREIGN INCOME

SOME COUNTRIES are kind enough to forego taxing foreign income entirely, even though they do tax income earned within their own territories. For this reason, these countries are sometimes referred to as "territorial tax" countries because they only tax income that was produced in their own territory. You could say that these countries are the silver medalists when it comes to their tax laws.

Countries That Do Not Tax Foreign Income

Latin America:

1. Costa Rica

2. Panama

3. Paraguay

4. Nicaragua

Europe:

5. Georgia

6. San Marino

7. Gibraltar

Asia:

8. Hong Kong

9. Macau

10. Malaysia

11. Singapore

12. Thailand

13. The Philippines

Many of the countries listed above are probably going to be in a sweet spot for most people. They are relatively attractive countries to live in and also, with the possible exception of Singapore, relatively affordable for most Americans living abroad. See Chapter 7 for our country-specific cost of living index.

Note that the mere fact that a country does not tax foreign income at all does not necessarily make it a favorable country from an overall tax perspective. This is because such countries may have other kinds of tax requirements to make up for their loss of income tax as a revenue source. Some of these other tax requirements might include such items as consumption taxes (as in VAT or sales tax), import tariffs, property taxes, social security contributions, transfer taxes, acquisition taxes, stamp taxes, gift taxes, estate taxes, net wealth taxes, net worth taxes, exit taxes and possibly even (though unlikely) pet, church and poll taxes. Make sure that you investigate each country thoroughly to find out what its taxation policies are and if any of those policies might rule out that country for you as a viable option.

If You Are Not Taxed on Foreign Income by Country X

As we mentioned in Chapter 1 as an answer to the Big Question, don't forget that just because you are not paying income tax in Country X, it does not necessarily mean that you do not have to pay any income tax anywhere at all. You may still be obligated to pay U.S. income taxes, provided you are viewed as a taxpayer by the U.S.

The good news is that, if you are not paying income tax on your foreign income (income that has a source that is outside Country X) to Country X, then you might only have to pay U.S. income tax on that "foreign income" (which might have a source inside the U.S. or anywhere else in the world).

The even better news is that paying U.S. income tax on that income, regardless of the source of that income, *while living abroad* might make you eligible to benefit from the Foreign Earned Income Exclusion (FEIE). If you are eligible for the FEIE, then you might be eligible for either the Foreign Housing Deduction or the Foreign Housing Exclusion. See Chapter 14 for more information.

Again, it doesn't matter if your foreign income has a U.S. source to be eligible for U.S. tax savings. The key is that you are earning it while living abroad.

For more resources and additional information to help you start an exciting new chapter in your life, please visit our website at www.AllPointsGuide.com.

5. COUNTRIES THAT TAX FOREIGN INCOME

THE REALITY IS THAT most countries tax foreign income. You could say that these countries are the bronze medalists when it comes to their tax laws. The good news is that most of the countries that do tax foreign income only tax the people that they view as "tax residents" on their foreign income. A tax resident is simply someone a country views as having enough factors tying them to its country that it decides it is fair to treat them as a taxpayer and require them to pay taxes. We will cover those factors in detail in this chapter and also on a country-by-country basis.

Note that nearly all countries (except those countries identified in Chapter 3) will tax you on income that you earn from a country's own sources, and they don't care if you are a tax resident or not, but there are also countries that will tax you on your worldwide income if they view you as a tax resident.

As an example of a country taxing you on money earned from sources within the country, if you run an AirBnB operation of just a single room in its country, then that country will likely tax you on the income derived from that AirBnB operation.

As an example of a country taxing you on worldwide income, a country that happens to be located in Asia or Europe might tax you on money you earn remotely from a company located in the United States if they view you as a tax resident of their country.

Each country has its own rules used to determine if someone is a tax resident. Sometimes those rules are simple, and it is relatively easy to determine if you qualify as a tax resident that is subject to tax on the foreign portion of your worldwide income or if you qualify as a nonresident foreigner that is not subject to tax on your foreign earnings.

Tie-breakers

If you do qualify as a tax resident of a country, that does not necessarily mean that you will be required to pay taxes to that country. If the country believes that you are also a tax resident of another country, such as the U.S., then there might be one or more tie-breaker tests used to determine which of the two countries gets the right to tax you on that foreign income. Often, such tie-breaker tests are written into the tax treaties between the U.S. and other countries.

Domestic Income

In any event, if you earn domestic income in these countries from domestic sources, know that you will likely be subject to tax on that specific income. For instance, if you run a restaurant in Country X, the money that you receive from those enterprises will likely be viewed as taxable income even if you personally aren't considered a tax resident by Country X.

If You Are Not Taxed on Foreign Income by Country X

As we mentioned in Chapter 1 as an answer to the Big Question, don't forget that just because you are not paying income tax in Country X, it does not necessarily mean that you do not have to pay any income tax anywhere at all. You may still be obligated to pay U.S. income taxes, provided you are viewed as a taxpayer by the U.S.

The good news is that, if you are not paying income tax on your foreign income (income that has a source that is outside Country X) to Country X, then you might only have to pay U.S. income tax on that "foreign income" (which might have a source inside the U.S. or anywhere else in the world).

The even better news is that paying U.S. income tax on that income, regardless of the source of that income, *while living abroad* might make you eligible to benefit from the Foreign Earned Income Exclusion (FEIE). If you are eligible for the FEIE, then you might be eligible for either the Foreign Housing Deduction or the Foreign Housing Exclusion. See Chapter 14 for more information.

Again, it doesn't matter if your foreign income has a U.S. source to be eligible for U.S. tax savings. The key is that you are earning it while living abroad.

Simple Rules

This chapter focuses on those countries that have relatively simple rules for determining whether or not you will be viewed as a tax resident for tax purposes and, therefore, subject to a tax on your foreign earnings. Before we review those countries, let us discuss various strategies you can employ in order to minimize the likelihood of being viewed by Country X as a tax resident.

STEPS YOU CAN TAKE TO AVOID BEING VIEWED AS A TAX RESIDENT

STAYING ON THE MOVE

Countries might be less inclined to tax foreign income if you spend half or less of the year in their country. If you are spending no more than, say, 90 days per year in a given country or maybe as much as 180 days per year, then certain countries are less likely to assert a tax on your foreign income.

This, arguably, gives the "digital nomad" lifestyle an advantage. This means that they MIGHT, depending upon a number of possible other factors, treat you as merely a tourist passing through who is not subject to taxation on your foreign income. Again, there are no guarantees that a country in this category will not assert that your foreign income is taxable by them.

"What about the other days of the year?"

Let's say you can only spend 182 days of the year in Country X. Where do you spend the remaining days of any given 12-month rolling period before returning to Country X?

For some people, they might choose to return home to the United States. Unfortunately, if you are a U.S. taxpayer seeking eligibility for the FEIE, the Foreign Housing Exclusion or the Foreign Housing Deduction, then returning to the U.S. might make you ineligible for any of those exclusions and/or deductions. This is because you need to make sure that you are satisfying the requirements of either the Bona Fide Residency Test or the Physical Presence Test (see Chapter 14 for more information) in order to maintain your eligibility for those exclusions and/or deductions.

You would, therefore, spend the other days in another country outside of the United States making sure that your foreign income will not be subject to tax in that other country.

Example: Let's Look at Germany

As an example of how this works, Germany states that it views people as tax residents if they spend 6 months or more out of a given tax year in Germany. In theory, therefore, if you only spend, say, 179 days out of a given tax year in Germany, it is unlikely that you will be viewed by Germany as a tax resident. Keep in mind that there are no guarantees about how a given country will treat you.

The Possible Advantage of Not Becoming a Resident or Citizen

Generally, if you take steps to become a temporary or permanent resident visa holder or citizen of one the countries in this category, or, if you successfully become a resident or citizen of one of the countries in this category, you will be increasing the risk of being treated as a tax resident. If you are treated as a tax resident, then you run the risk of being taxed on your foreign income by the country of which you seek to become a resident or citizen.

We are not telling you that you shouldn't become a resident or citizen of any of the countries in this category. There may be huge benefits in doing so. We are merely telling you that there could be a downside if you do so from a tax perspective (see Chapter 14 for more information on the tax issues involved).

In some countries, becoming a resident or citizen may not result in you becoming a tax resident. You need to do some research to find out if any particular country will view you as a tax resident if you become a resident or citizen of that country.

It depends on the rules of a specific rules of a country. We recommend that you do research on any country you are considering living in and consult with a tax professional in that country that specializes in advising foreigners.

Possible Advantage of Short-term Renting

If you are a U.S. taxpayer, and you want to pay into the Social Security system to maximize your benefits, or if you plan to take advantage of the Foreign Earned Income Exclusion and possibly an exclusion or deduction of your housing expenses, then you may want to take the following measures to minimize your risk of being treated as a tax resident of Country X: Rent a home in Country X for not more than you are allowed per 12-month rolling period and seek foreign (outside of

Country X) sources of income. Renting for short-terms on AirBnB and VRBO would be ideal for this.

Example: You can only stay 183 days in Mexico in a rolling 12-month period without (everything else being equal) being considered a tax resident. Just prior to day 183, therefore, you leave and go to Costa Rica for 3 months and then Colombia for three months for before returning to Mexico.

The Possible Advantage of Having Vital Interests Outside Country X

You may be less likely to be taxed by certain countries if your vital interests are outside of those countries. "Vital interests" can be defined as sources of income, owning property or assets of a particular country, registering for social security in a particular country, sending your children to a school in a particular country, etc.

As an example: You might, therefore, be less likely to be treated as a Country X tax resident if your assets and the sources of your income are situated outside of Country X. If you are a U.S. citizen working remotely in this example, then it is possible that that most of your income will be coming from U.S. sources and, thus, the foreign country or countries that you are living in might be less likely to assert that your income is subject to their taxation.

THE POSSIBLE DISADVANTAGES

It is important to note that not purchasing a home in Country X may come with some drawbacks (see the section on renting vs. buying in

Chapter 13 for a further discussion of the potential advantages and disadvantages that might come with either buying or renting a home in Country X). The impact of any such drawbacks might outweigh any potential tax benefits. This is a judgment call that you are going to have to make.

NO GUARANTEES

There are no guarantees that taking any step mentioned in this book will prevent you from being treated as a taxpayer of Country X on your foreign income. Keep in mind, therefore, that there is a certain amount of risk of having your income taxed by Country X no matter what country or countries you choose to live in. We are merely providing you with information that might minimize the risk of being treated as a taxpayer on your foreign income.

Also, our review of each country is not intended to be comprehensive and 100% inclusive of all the rules of each country. It is important that you do your own research and consult with a tax professional that specializes in the taxation of foreigners in each country that you are considering living in.

A COUNTRY-BY-COUNTRY REVIEW

In most countries, the chance that you will be taxed on foreign income is more likely if you are viewed as a tax resident of that country. Below is a list of countries and what might decrease your chances of being deemed a tax resident (and, thus, less likely to be taxed on foreign income) in each.

IMPORTANT NOTE

Some countries are **not** included on the list below either because they are already named in this book as not taxing foreign income or because their rules on tax residency are very complex and do not lend themselves to a simple test. If a country has complex tax laws, we recommend that you consult with a tax professional in that country to help you figure out if you will be deemed a tax resident if you live there. Some of these countries with complex rules might include the following: Australia, Israel, Mexico, New Zealand, Sweden, Switzerland and the United Kingdom.

Argentina: If you haven't lived in Argentina for twelve months or more and you have not applied to become a resident, you might be *less likely* to be considered a tax resident.

Austria: If you haven't lived in Austria for six months or more within a given tax year (these days do not have to be consecutive provided they occur in the same 12-month period) or applied for and received residency, then you might be *less likely* to be considered a tax resident.

Belgium: If you do not obtain a work visa or an entrepreneurship visa in Belgium, then you may be *less likely* to be considered a resident.

Brazil: If you aren't in Brazil for more than 183 days within any 12-month period (do not have to be consecutive) and you do not have permanent residency, then you may be *less likely* to be considered a resident.

Chile: If you do not live in Chile for 180 consecutive days in one year or live in Chile for 180 nonconsecutive days per year for two years, then you may be *less likely* to be considered a resident.

Denmark: If you do not stay in Denmark for more than six consecutive months and you do not have a permanent home situated in Denmark, then you may be *less likely* to be considered a resident.

Estonia: If you do not live in Estonia for 183 or more days during any one tax period (may be nonconsecutive), then you may be *less likely* to be considered a resident.

Finland: If you do not stay in Finland for more than six months (may be nonconsecutive) and you do not have a permanent home situated in Finland, then you may be *less likely* to be considered a resident.

France: If your primary residence isn't in France, your primary employment or professional activity isn't derived from France or activities that take place in France or you haven't spent at least 183 days in France in a single year (may be nonconsecutive), then you may be *less likely* to be considered a resident.

Germany: If you do not have a "habitual abode" that you've lived in for at least six months out of a given tax year and you do not own a home in Germany, then you may be *less likely* to be considered a resident.

Greece: If you don't spend 183 days in any 12-month period in Greece (may be nonconsecutive) or aren't deemed to have a habitual abode or "vital interests" in Greece, then you may be *less likely* to be considered a resident. The definition of vital interests may include the following: owning significant property in Greece, registering for Greek social security or sending your children to a Greek school.

Ireland: If you don't reside in Ireland for 183 days (may be nonconsecutive) or more during one tax year or you don't reside for a total of 280 days or more (may be nonconsecutive) in Ireland over the last two tax years, then you may be *less likely* to be considered a resident.

Italy: If you're not present in Italy for more than 183 days in any 12-month rolling period (these days do not have to be consecutive), then you may be *less likely* to be considered a resident.

Norway: If you have not lived in Norway for more than 183 days (may be nonconsecutive) in a calendar year or more than 270 days in a 36-month time frame (may be nonconsecutive), then you may be *less likely* to be considered a resident.

Peru: If you don't live in Peru for 183 days (may be nonconsecutive) out of the calendar year, then you may be *less likely* to be considered a resident.

Spain: If you don't spend more than 183 days (may be nonconsecutive) in Spain during a calendar year, you don't have business or economic interests centered in Spain and neither your spouse nor your underage children are deemed to be tax residents of Spain, then you may be *less likely* to be considered a resident. Moreover, even if you fail one of the above tests, you may be less likely to be considered a resident if you can prove that you are a tax resident of another country.

For more resources and additional information to help you start an exciting new chapter in your life, please visit our website at www.AllPointsGuide.com.

6. QUALITY OF LIFE

BELOW ARE THE TOP 57 countries in the world viewed to be the best countries on Earth in which to live. They are determined to be more favorable than the countries below them on the basis of the following: each country's (a) quality of life, (b) culture, (c) spirit of entrepreneurship, (d) influence in the world and (e) possibilities for adventure.

This list focuses on larger countries. Small island countries and microstates, for instance, might have been ignored.

COUNTRIES WITH THE BEST QUALITY OF LIFE
(starting with the best overall)

1. Switzerland	20. South Korea	39. Costa Rica
2. Germany	21. UAE	40. Indonesia
3. Canada	22. Austria	41. South Africa
4. United States	23. Ireland	42. Morocco
5. Sweden	24. Luxembourg	43. Czechia
6. Japan	25. Greece	44. Croatia
7. Australia	26. Portugal	45. Philippines
8. United Kingdom	27. Brazil	46. Vietnam
9. France	28. Thailand	47. Hungary
10. Denmark	29. Qatar	48. Chile
11. New Zealand	30. Turkey	49. Peru
12. Netherlands	31. India	50. Dominican Republic
13. Norway	32. Poland	51. Colombia
14. Italy	33. Mexico	52. Panama
15. Finland	34. Saudi Arabia	53. Romania
16. Spain	35. Egypt	54. Sri Lanka
17. China	36. Israel	55. Estonia
18. Belgium	37. Argentina	56. Ecuador
19. Singapore	38. Malaysia	57. Paraguay

"Can I live in Country X on my Social Security income alone?"

This is often the first question that people ask regarding "the expat life" in general. In order to answer this age-old question, we would need to know (a) exactly how much you are receiving from Social Security and any other sources, (b) exactly where in Country X you want to live, (c) how frugally you are willing to live, (d) how much health insurance you want to purchase and (e) how much of a safety cushion you want to have. The safety cushion is something people do not always budget for, but you should be setting some money aside each month for a rainy, and possibly torrential, day.

Whatever your choices, make sure you are paying into Country X's public healthcare system if you are eligible for it and possibly a long-term international health insurance plan such as one by CIGNA Global, GeoBlue, William Russell, or another provider. Even if health insurance raises your costs, it could save your life, and your finances, in the future in the event of a catastrophic injury or illness.

If you are eligible for Medicare in the United States, then it makes sense that you are paying, at minimum for Part A, Part B Part C and Part D coverage (and make sure your Part C a/k/a Medicare Advantage plan has no maximum coverage for emergent or urgent care in Country X). This is something to discuss with your insurance broker. Paying for full Medicare coverage makes sense even if you are living outside the U.S. full-time with no plans to ever return. It's a good "insurance policy" to have.

A Note on Medicare Part B

Consider accepting Part B coverage, even if you think it will not help you in Country X, for three reasons.

First, Part B is a prerequisite for getting Part C (Medicare Advantage) coverage which may help you in the event of an emergency or urgent care need while in Country X.

Second, even if you do not need Part B coverage now, you might need it in coming years, especially if you do not have IMSS coverage or private international coverage like CIGNA Global, GeoBlue, William Russell, or another provider.

Third, if you decline it now, you could face significant penalties for adding it months or years after your Medicare Part A coverage starts.

☆ ☆ ☆ ☆ ☆

For more resources and additional information to help you start an exciting new chapter in your life, please visit our website at www.AllPointsGuide.com.

7. COST OF LIVING

FINDING OUT WHAT THINGS COST in Country X will help you to avoid surprises when you arrive there.

Let's take a look at what countries have the lowest cost of living. Then look for any countries that overlap your other lists: countries with a favorable tax policy, countries that are easy to access and countries with the best quality of life.

COUNTRIES WITH THE LOWEST COST OF LIVING

(starting with the most affordable)

1	Egypt	35	Georgia	68	Cyprus
2	India	36	Montenegro	69	Yemen
3	Colombia	37	China	70	Uruguay
4	Nepal	38	Hungary	71	UAE
5	Sri Lanka	39	Guatemala	72	Italy
6	Ukraine	40	Bulgaria	73	Malta
7	Kyrgyzstan	41	Thailand	74	UK
8	Uzbekistan	42	Mauritius	75	Germany
9	Algeria	43	El Salvador	76	Sweden
10	Kazakhstan	44	Chile	77	Japan
11	Turkey	45	Slovakia	78	Belgium
12	Paraguay	46	Cambodia	79	Lebanon
13	Morocco	47	Portugal	80	Austria
14	Argentina	48	Croatia	81	Canada
15	Indonesia	49	Jordan	82	Finland
16	Bolivia	50	Kuwait	83	Netherlands
17	Moldova	51	Guyana	84	France
18	Kenya	52	Oman	85	South Korea
19	Peru	53	Belize	86	Ireland
20	Philippines	54	Panama	87	United States
21	Brazil	55	Costa Rica	88	New Zealand
22	Malaysia	56	Lithuania	89	Luxembourg
23	Bosnia	57	Czechia	90	Australia
24	Ecuador	58	Spain	91	Hong Kong
25	Belarus	59	Slovenia	92	Israel
26	Vietnam	60	Latvia	93	Denmark
27	Nicaragua	61	Trinidad	94	Iceland
28	Serbia	62	Jamaica	95	Singapore
29	Mexico	63	Taiwan	96	Norway
30	Albania	64	Greece	97	Barbados
31	Romania	65	Estonia	98	Bahamas
32	South Africa	66	Maldives	99	Caymans
33	Fiji	67	Brunei	100	Switzerland
34	Poland			101	Bermuda

8. GAINING ACCESS TO A COUNTRY

A COUNTRY MIGHT BE PERFECT for you on paper, but if its government won't let you in, its perfection does you very little good. Each country has its own set of requirements for people that seek entry into its country, and those requirements tend to be dynamic and can change frequently. Make sure that when you are researching countries, you also look at their tourism/visa rules and restrictions. For a very thorough look at the requirements of Mexico, please see our book All Points Guide Living in Mexico.

COUNTRIES THAT GIVE AUTOMATIC ACCESS TO HOLDERS OF U.S. PASSPORTS

Wikipedia maintains a list of countries that holders of U.S. passports can access in most cases automatically. Here is the link:

https://en.m.wikipedia.org/wiki/Visa_requirements_for_United_States_citizens

Here is a brief summary of selected countries in that list:

COUNTRY	TIME ALLOTTED
Argentina	90 days (extendable to 180)
Australia	90 days
Austria	90 days
Bahamas	8 months
Barbados	6 months
Belgium	90 days
Belize	90 days
Brazil	90 days
Bulgaria	90 days
Canada	6 months
Colombia	90 days (extendable to 180)
Costa Rica	90 days
Croatia	90 days
Cyprus	90 days
Czechia (Czech Republic)	90 days
Denmark	90 days
Dominican Republic	30 days (extendable up to 90)

COUNTRY	TIME ALLOTTED
Ecuador	90 days (extendable up to 180)
Finland	90 days
France	90 days
Georgia	1 year
Germany	90 days
Greece	90 days
Hungary	3 months
Iceland	90 days
India	180 days
Indonesia	30 days
Ireland	3 months
Israel	3 months
Italy	90 days
Japan	3 months
S. Korea	90 days
Kyrgyzstan	60 days
Latvia	180 days
Liechtenstein	90 days
Lithuania	90 days
Luxembourg	90 days
Malaysia	3 months
Malta	90 days
Marshall Islands	unlimited
Mauritius	60 days
Mexico	up to 180 days
Micronesia	unlimited
Moldova	90 days

COUNTRY	TIME ALLOTTED
Monaco	90 days
Morocco	3 months
Nepal	90 days
Netherlands	90 days
New Zealand	3 months
Norway	90 days
Palau	1 year
Panama	180 days
Paraguay	90 days
Peru	90 days
Philippines	30 days
Poland	90 days
Portugal	90 days
Romania	90 days
St. Kitts and Nevis	1 months
Serbia	90 days
Seychelles	3 months
Singapore	90 days
Slovakia	90 days
Slovenia	90 days
Solomon Islands	3 months
South Africa	90 days
Spain	90 days
Sweden	90 days
Switzerland	90 days
Taiwan	90 days
Thailand	90 days

COUNTRY	TIME ALLOTTED
Trinidad & Tobago	90 days
Tunisia	90 days
Turkey	3 months
United Kingdom	6 months
Uruguay	3 months
Vietnam	30 days

TRAVEL REQUIREMENTS IN EUROPE

Currently, U.S. citizens need to limit their stay in most European "Schengen-zone countries" to 90 days within any 180-day period (the current limit). Those seeking to stay longer in a country or travel for purposes such as work or study require a visa.

Schengen-zone countries include the following countries: Austria, Belgium, Croatia, Czechia (a/k/a the Czech Republic), Denmark, Estonia, Finland, France, Germany, Greece, Hungary, Italy, Latvia, Lithuania, Luxembourg, Malta, the Netherlands, Poland, Portugal, Slovakia, Slovenia, Spain and Sweden.

What digital nomads sometimes do to avoid violating this rule is this: They stay in a Schengen-zone country for three months and then stay in a non-Schengen-zone country in Europe for the next three months and then rotate between the two *types* of countries.

Here are the non-Schengen-zone countries that happen to also be members of the EU: Bulgaria, Romania, Cyprus and Ireland.

Here are the non-Schengen-zone countries in Europe that are not in the EU: Albania, Armenia, Azerbaijan, Belarus, Bosnia & Herzegovina, Macedonia, Moldova, Montenegro, Serbia and the United Kingdom.

You can stay in non-Schengen-zone countries from either list without violating the "90 days within 180" rule.

For example, you could stay in Spain (Schengen) for three months, followed by a stay in Ireland (non-Schengen) for three months, followed by a stay in Germany (Schengen) for three months, followed by a stay in Serbia (non-Schengen) for three months.

Note that travelers to any Schengen-zone country may have to register with the European Travel Information and Authorization System (ETIAS) starting as early as 2024. ETIAS may prove to be similar to the Electronic System for Travel Authorization (ESTA) already used in the United States.

ETIAS will have very little impact on most travelers. The process will involve a quick online application and a €7.00 credit card payment. The European Commission states that "ETIAS will be a simple, fast and visitor-friendly system, which will, in more than 95% of cases, result in a positive answer within a few minutes."

The ETIAS authorization will be valid for unlimited entries within a three-year period (or until the date of the applicant's passport expiry, whichever is sooner) so travelers who frequent Europe won't need to apply every time they visit. Without a visa (ETIAS is not a visa), U.S. citizens will still need to limit their travel to 90 days within any 180-day period (the current limit). As noted above, those seeking to stay longer in a country or travel for purposes such as work or study require a visa.

ETIAS authorization will be needed for travel to any country that is part of the Schengen Borders Agreement, as well as countries that are European Free Trade Association (EFTA) Members, European Microstates with Open Borders, as well as Future Schengen Members ("Home ETIAS Countries"). This includes: Austria, Belgium, Czechia (a/k/a the Czech Republic), Denmark, Estonia, Finland, France,

Germany, Greece, Hungary, Iceland, Italy, Latvia, Liechtenstein, Lithuania, Luxembourg, Malta, Netherlands, Norway, Poland, Portugal, Slovakia, Slovenia, Spain, Sweden, and Switzerland.

THE POTENTIAL DOWNSIDE OF BECOMING A RESIDENT OR CITIZEN OF COUNTRY X

While becoming a temporary or permanent resident or a citizen of Country X is generally a good thing for many people, we must mention that there is one potential downside in becoming a resident or a citizen of Country X that you should know about. If you become a resident or citizen of Country X, you may be viewed as what is called a "tax resident" of Country X.

Becoming a tax resident simply means that Country X would have the right to tax you on all your income including your foreign income, not just what you earn from Country X sources.

We are not telling you that you shouldn't become a resident or citizen of Country X. You might be able to achieve huge personal gains, benefits and freedom by becoming a resident or citizen of Country X. We are merely telling you that there could be a downside from a tax perspective if you go that route.

POTENTIAL DRAWBACKS

There are **two** main potential drawbacks of being taxed by Country X on foreign income.

First, it might mean you will not be paying into the U.S. system to the maximum extent possible based on your total income. Not paying in might mean that your future Social Security benefits will be reduced.

Second, it might make you ineligible for the Foreign Earned Income Exclusion, the Foreign Housing Deduction and/or the Foreign Housing Exclusion (see Chapter 14 for more information about these tax issues).

When you are dealing with foreign bureaucracies, keep in mind that their approach might be different than the approach used by bureaucracies in the United States. One key difference is the format for presenting dates, such as your date of birth.

Day/Month/Year

This is a small matter, but it can have major consequences. Make sure that when you're supplying dates on any form provided by most governments you will most likely be using a Day/Month/Year or DD/MM/YYYY format. So, if you were born on May 9, 1980, you would enter your date of birth as 09/05/1980.

Furthermore, you want to ensure that all the information that you present about yourself to be consistent and make everything match what is on your passport exactly.

TYPES OF VISAS

If you are visiting or living in Country X without a valid visa, you would be facing fines, ejection from the country and even detention in a holding facility. Your stay in the detention facility might only be for a few days or it could be for weeks or even months. In short, we urge you to not view your obligation to be in Country X legally as a frivolous matter.

TOURIST VISA

The most common document that people use to visit many countries is the tourist visa, which could grant you a number of months but likely not more than 6 months at a time. For digital nomads, this might be sufficient. But if you are looking to settle down somewhere, this will likely not a long-term solution for people that want to live in Country X.

Many countries grant automatic entry to citizens and/or residents of the United States, Great Britain, Northern Ireland, Canada, Japan and the Schengen Treaty Area.

If, however, you are coming from any country other than one of the countries identified above, then you may need to obtain preauthorization from a consulate (which is often embedded within an embassy) of many countries. Also, there are some countries that do not offer preferential treatment to United States, Great Britain, Northern Ireland, Canada, Japan and the Schengen Treaty Area.

"What is an apostille and why would I need such a thing?"

An apostille is similar to a notarization in that it certifies the authenticity of a signature on a document. In accordance with an international convention, an apostille is obtained directly from a country's applicable governmental agency.

Some countries will require that you provide them with items, such as birth certificates, that have been apostilled. In some cases, you may need to provide items that have not only been apostilled but also translated by a certified translator.

FINDING A BASIS FOR RESIDENCY

If you would like to stay in Country X for a longer period than the number of days or months allotted to tourists, then you must find some basis for being granted residency. Let us explore some of the most typical foundations for being granted a residency visa.

• Owning a House in Country X

If you own a house in some countries, free of any mortgage or other liens, then you can apply for temporary residency. The assessed value of the house may need to be equal to or greater than a value required under the qualification rules.

• Family Connections

If you have certain types of family connections in Country, you may be able to apply for residency on the basis of family unity. An example of this would be that if your spouse is a citizen of Country X, then Country X will probably provide a pathway for you to gain resident status within Country X.

Note that some countries will not only give you a visa but actual citizenship and a passport if you simply have family lineage from that country. In some cases, countries will even look back at a time when your ancestors had citizenship even if it means skipping multiple generations of your ancestors that did *not* have citizenship. For instance, there is a law in Spain that enables Sephardic Jews who are descendants of those expelled from Spain in the 15th century to obtain Spanish citizenship without renouncing their current citizenship and without requiring residency in Spain.

• Making a Capital (Monetary) Investment in Country X

In some cases, if you make a capital investment in some countries, you may be granted a path to residency in that country. An example of this would be depositing a certain amount in a Country X bank account or buying a certain amount of stock in Country X companies.

Some countries require investments equal to hundreds of thousands of U.S. dollars. Other countries require much less. For instance, Ecuador offered an Investor Visa in exchange for a minimum investment of $42,500 USD in 2022.

• Local Job Offer (Employer as Sponsor)

Having an employer in Country X offer you a job can be a pathway towards residency. It can, however, undercut your intentions to earn money from sources outside of Country X so that you aren't taxed by Country X. For U.S. taxpayers, taking a job from a Country X employer would make it unlikely that you could benefit from something like the Foreign Earned Income Exclusion. This might be a worthwhile tradeoff for some people, though. It all depends on how it meshes with your short-term and long-term goals.

• Humanitarian Grounds and Political Asylum

It's possible to apply for residency in some countries on humanitarian grounds or under the auspices of political asylum. These are very specialized applications, and you should contact your nearest immigration office in Country X for guidance and advice.

While, at first blush, it might seem unlikely that someone from the United States would ever qualify for a humanitarian visa, you might be surprised. Let's say that you're an Asian woman, and there has been a recent spate of assaults and even homicides against Asian women in the United States. You could testify that you feel your life is threatened in the United States and, for that reason, you seek asylum in Country X. There is no guarantee that such a claim would be successful, but that kind of a claim might be convincing enough to gain a visa from some countries.

• Special Programs and Procedures

In addition to everything mentioned above, there is always a chance that a country will have a special program that fits your needs. A common special program is a special program to accommodate digital nomads. Such programs tend to require that you have a letter from an employer to guarantee your work. Obviously, this doesn't do much to help freelancers. But it pays to do research and see if any such programs exist.

FINANCIAL SOLVENCY VISAS

Some, but not all, countries offer visas on the basis of you having the financial means to provide for yourself. These kinds of solvency visas are sometimes tied to age requirements as they are targeted towards retirees.

In some countries, like Mexico, you can obtain either a temporary visa or a permanent visa based on a demonstrating financial ability to pay for your own expenses while in Country X.

> ## NOTE
>
> You might be eligible for the "retiree" visa even if you aren't retired so long as you have the required assets or income stream and perhaps over some age that is deemed adequate. It all depends on the country's own policies. Working with an immigration attorney from Country X when seeking a long-term visa might be a great idea.

PROVIDING NOTICE OF CHANGES

If you hold a residency visa, you may be required to report any change of your status to an immigration office if there is any change to one or more of the following:

• address
• marriage
• divorce
• death of your spouse
• any change to your income sources in Country X such as a termination, change in employer, etc.

APPLYING FOR CITIZENSHIP IN COUNTRY X

If you intend to apply for Country X citizenship and become naturalized, you may first need to obtain legal residency and then apply for citizenship after the qualifying period.

Depending upon which countries you currently have already established citizenship, either by birth or naturalization, you might have to surrender your country of origin's passport and renounce your prior citizenship when you acquire your Country X nationality. Fortunately, this is rare. Most countries, such as the United States, allow their citizens to hold dual or multiple citizenships.

You should check in with competent legal and financial advisers about the implications that your naturalization may have on your personal and business tax affairs.

NOTE: Becoming a citizen will likely expose you to having your foreign income taxed by your adoptive country.

RENOUNCING CITIZENSHIP IN THE U.S.

Many newly naturalized citizens of foreign countries think that, by renouncing their citizenship in their country of origin, they will save a fortune in taxes. For several reasons, we do not generally recommend voluntarily renouncing your citizenship in the U.S. whether or not your tax obligations will be improved. Ultimately, though, it's your choice to make.

The first reason we recommend that you maintain citizenship in your country of origin is to minimize the possibility of being denied coverage for a public benefits program in your country of origin at some point by any applicable public or private insurance provider. You may want to keep this option open in case you require medical or skilled nursing attention in your country of origin.

The second reason you should consider maintaining your citizenship is that even if you could convince the state and/or federal tax collection services back home that you are no longer a taxpayer after renouncing your citizenship, your taxpaying obligations would not end. You would simply start paying tax to Country X instead of to your country of origin.

Your marginal tax rate might not be any better in Country X than it was in the U.S. To put current U.S. tax obligations in perspective, a U.S. taxpayer living in a state with no state income tax might be viewed quite enviably by many heavily taxed Europeans who might see the United States as a tax haven compared to their own countries. U.S. marginal tax rates have dropped over the years.

The third reason to maintain your citizenship is that it might be possible, if there is a double taxation treaty between your country of origin and Country X, to pay your taxes in Country X without paying taxes in the U.S. This is because you would get a tax credit to use in your country of origin when you have paid your taxes in Country X (see our discussion of double taxation treaties in Chapter 14 for reference). But take note once again that paying taxes in Country X means that you may not be able to benefit from the Foreign Earned Income Exclusion, the Foreign Housing Deduction and/or the Foreign Housing Exclusion.

By maintaining your citizenship in your country of origin, any double taxation treaty between Country X and the U.S. still applies and you are not necessarily taxed a second time by Country X on the tax liability you already paid in the U.S., even if you are now a citizen of Country X, as well. This all pivots on your ability to apply tax credits paid in one country towards taxes otherwise owed in another correctly (see Chapter 14 for more information). Due to the trickiness of all of this, we recommend you work with accounts in all applicable countries to make sure that you have fulfilled your tax obligations to each country that might consider you a tax resident.

The fourth reason to maintain your citizenship is that you might need to return to your country of origin for reasons that you cannot currently anticipate, and you would not want to face the requirement of procuring a visa to get back inside the United States.

One of the most common reasons for a prolonged or permanent return to one's country of origin is that a friend or family member back home becomes sick and needs your care. This is something that could potentially happen to you even if you intended to never return.

The fifth reason to maintain your citizenship is the potential of having to surrender the advantages that come with being a citizen of your home country, such as possibly having a top-tier passport that might have advantages over a Country X passport.

The sixth reason to maintain your citizenship is that the United States, might impose an expatriation or "exit" tax on you if you are deemed to be a high-net-worth individuals when you renounce either your citizenship or long-term residency, as the case may be.

We, therefore, recommend maintaining dual citizenship *in most cases* rather than renouncing your citizenship in your country of origin. This assumes, of course, that the U.S. will allow you to be a dual citizen with Country X and, simultaneously, that Country X will allow you to be a dual citizen with the U.S.

☆ ☆ ☆ ☆ ☆

For more resources and additional information to help you start an exciting new chapter in your life, please visit our website at www.AllPointsGuide.com.

9. HOW TO AFFORD LIFE ABROAD

THERE ARE MANY REASONS that draw people to foreign countries, but one of the most compelling inducements is how affordable many foreign countries are compared to the United States. If you are able to, say, halve your costs but maintain your current income levels, you are essentially improving your standard of living by a factor of 2. There is a fancy term for taking dollars earned in the U.S. and using them in a relatively affordable country, namely, GEOGRAPHIC ARBITRAGE.

If you are working or not yet fully retired, you have many options for earning money. Some of these options will involve working remotely (such as by working as a freelancer for clients back in the U.S., Canada and Europe) and other options will involve working in Country X, such as running an AirBnB operation in a city in Country X. Note that drawing income from Country X sources may mean that you will not be able to benefit from the Foreign Earned Income Exclusion, the Foreign Housing Deduction and/or the Foreign Housing Exclusion

As we will discuss in Chapter 14, it is important to note that working remotely rather than drawing on the economy of Country X can have serious tax advantages, especially if Country X does not view you as a "tax resident."

The ultimate decision about how you draw your income, however, is up to you. We are merely presenting the information you need to make an informed decision. What is right for one person may not be right for another.

GEOGRAPHIC ARBITRAGE

The heart of moving from a country that has a relatively high cost of living to a country that has a significantly lower cost of living is referred to as geographic arbitrage. While the phrase might sound very heady and technical, geographic arbitrage is a surprisingly simple concept to understand. It just means that one can seek ways to gain an advantage by earning money in an economy that pays relatively higher wages and then spending that money in a country in which the cost of living is relatively lower.

To put it another way, geographic arbitrage may allow you to live luxuriously on money that might not have gone very far in the country where you earned it due to that country's higher cost of living. In a sense, you are straddling two economies so that you may maximize the value of your money.

If you are fully retired, geographic arbitrage would consist of (1) keeping the lion's share of your cash, cash equivalents, investments and other assets in your country of origin "working" for you by producing growth and/or income and then (2) living on the money your money produces for you in a low-cost environment.

You can then draw on the money produced by your cash, cash equivalents, investments and other assets by transferring the cash that you need from your country of origin to your bank account in Country X, preferably transferring your money at a time when your original currency is at its peak strength against the currency of Country X.

EARN MONEY "BACK HOME" WHILE ABROAD

Possibly the best way to make money while living in Country X is to continue in your current job in the United States while you are living abroad or simply do any other US-based work remotely.

There could be substantial tax savings available to you if you are working remotely while living abroad. Read Chapter 14 for a discussion on tax issues and check with tax professionals that specialize in the tax issues that are specific to expats and digital nomads before you do anything along these lines.

We learned recently about a gentleman who wanted to work for his U.S. employer remotely in Mexico. He contacted his employer's human resources department and they set up a subsidiary company in Mexico just for him. And the subsidiary set up a Mexican payroll service just for him. His employer was well intentioned, but this idea was disastrous from a tax point of view because it ruined his opportunity to treat his income from his U.S. employer as excluded income under the Foreign Earned Income Exclusion (FEIE) on his U.S. tax returns. FEIE income is either not taxed or is largely untaxed. Instead of benefiting from the FEIE, he is paying Mexican income taxes which are somewhat comparable to U.S. income taxes. Continuing to be treated as a U.S. tax resident but filing for the FEIE might have yielded a much better result (see Chapter 14). He may have jeopardized his eligibility for either the Foreign Housing Deduction or the Foreign Housing Exclusion.

Important Questions to Ask About Working

Before you engage in any kind of commercial activity while in Country X, first check with your tax and legal professionals that are qualified to practice in Country X to find out if your efforts might be incurring or creating any Country X tax liability associated with your work and find out what the tax reporting requirements might be.

Work Your Current Job Remotely

If you are currently employed, talk to your employer about working remotely. And then do your job from Country X.

Work Any Regular Job Remotely

Think about all the jobs you may have had in the past: perhaps you have been a designer, teacher, newspaper editor, translator, etc., and then think about the possibility of doing that job remotely. Check a website like Indeed.com and find out if there are any positions available for doing that work remotely.

Build a portfolio that demonstrates your competence even if it means doing mock-ups for free. You might even need to offer your services for free or a low price to get your start and build up reviews and customers. Freelancing may require an increased effort to individualize your communications with clients to set yourself apart from the pack.

If you cannot do the kind of work you are doing now for your current employer or customers O R if you need to supplement that work, below is a list of ideas for you to consider. If you are interested in learning more about any of them, we recommend that you look at some YouTube tutorial videos that will tell you more about how to pursue each possible source of income.

If you need ideas, allow us to present the A-to-Zs of freelancing immediately below.

A. SELL YOUR ART & ILLUSTRATIONS

For marketing purposes, you might want to come up with a brand for your artwork. Once you have a brand, you have a few options for selling your artwork:

• Print-on-demand (POD) is a common way for artists to earn money online. Many individuals have adopted this business model as a way to monetize their ideas and designs. It is a good option because there is no inventory to maintain. An inventory can be a very costly component of traditional print businesses. Additionally, the production and delivery is outsourced, further reducing your costs.

You are essentially selling your own custom products that use your brand or logo or simply your own words and designs. And if you have graphic design skills, this might be a great way to put them into practice.

You can choose to have your designs placed on a select number of specific items or on a wide range of products. Most print-on-demand companies offer products such as mugs, tote bags and, of course, t-shirts.

You can really reduce costs if you are marketing your products through your existing social marketing sites, such as Pinterest and Instagram.

Print your designs on everything from socks to laptop cases to sneakers.

• Sell canvasses and other kinds of artwork on your website, your own Etsy and Society6 shops, and potentially retail stores like Target and Home Goods.

Using stock images and software like Adobe Illustrator and artificial intelligence (AI) allows even people with no formal training in art to create works of art.

One strategy for creating artwork is to not make any art until it is ordered. This allows you to customize your artwork based on customer input, and it also means you don't have to worry about costly inventory or wasted efforts.

• Promote your art and your brand using social networking sites: Go on TikTok or Instagram trying to find trending videos, and then put your own spin on those trends to advertise your shop.

• In addition to Etsy sales, you can earn additional money by licensing your artwork non-exclusively on platforms like Society6, which you can set up for free. The drawback is that you only get a 10% commission on the products you sell there.

B. CREATE AND SELL GREETING CARDS ONLINE

The best way to manufacture and market your own line of greeting cards is to identify a niche market that is being underserved and then designing cards for that demographic. For instance, you can sell thank you cards that would be perfect for dentists to send to their patients thanking them for their patronage.

There are online graphic tools like Photoshop and Canva that you can use to design your own cards. They should make it simple to assemble attractive cards that will make your customers feel like they are buying something only a Hallmark or an American Greetings could have put together. Little do they know that it's your own cottage business.

Once you have designed a card, you can use a print-on-demand service like Printify to produce physical cards, and then you can sell that card on a wide variety of the sales channels such as Shopify, Etsy and Squarespace.

C. MAKE MONEY WITH AFFILIATE MARKETING

Affiliate marketing is one of the best ways to make money online. Affiliate marketing allows you to select companies from a vast range of companies to partner with, including such companies as eBay Partner Network, Amazon Associates and the Uber Affiliate Program, that you truly believe in and know will add value to people's lives.

If you're a savvy marketer, you can earn a commission from sales by promoting retail products, software, apps, etc. While a single commission might seem like small potatoes, keep in mind that you can be an affiliate for several brands and include several affiliate URLs on a single blog post. Also, you can build your audience, readers and followers, so that there will be more clicks on your affiliate links.

The best way to do this is to build out a blog with several pages of high-quality content, thus creating an asset you can call your own. Then embed affiliate URLs strategically throughout your blog posts to drive traffic to your affiliates' websites.

D. START A YOUTUBE CHANNEL

Even if you have no experience in front or behind a camera, this is something you should at least consider doing to make money.

This isn't to say that everyone can make a lot of money on YouTube. There are many people who have wholeheartedly tried but have not made a single dime on YouTube.

If you want to give this a try, your best bet is to find a niche market that is being underserved by YouTube and then develop a strong, loyal following. For example, you can create cooking tutorials, review products, teach skills or anything else you think people would enjoy that isn't being properly represented.

Many people form the United States living in Country X have travel channels where they show what life is like for them in Country X. There seems to be a real demand for it. Best of all, you would essentially be getting compensated for living the life you love.

Create pithy headlines to grab people's attention and then add keywords in your description to optimize for YouTube algorithmic "engines." Once you have reached the 1,000-subscriber milestone, you can officially monetize your channel with YouTube ads.

Be sure to ask people to like your video and to follow you. Then place teasers up front that will keep people watching until the end. The more time people spend watching one of your videos, the more you, in theory, might get paid.

E. BECOME A YOUTUBE EDITOR

It might surprise you to learn that editing YouTube videos pays. A busy, experienced editor can make $80,000 per year on average; however, an editor typically makes about $50,000 in the first year or two.

You will need to learn to use a video editor like Final Cut Pro, iMovie or Adobe Premiere Pro. You can take a low-cost course on using a video editor at udemy.com or elsewhere on the Internet.

You will need to use a website like storyblocks.com for stock video that you can cut into the videos you are editing.

Once you have received some training and have done some test videos for practice, you can advertise your skills on sites like Fiverr, Upwork, Guru or Freelancer and hope to get paying customers for your services.

Building a personal brand can also help you make money online. Amazingly, soccer star Cristiano Ronaldo charges between $880,00 and $1 million USD, on average, for a sponsored Instagram post. While it may seem like reality stars, singers and athletes are the biggest influencers, keep in mind that even smaller-scale influencers can make more money today than they did a few years back.

To begin your journey as an influencer, you will first need to build a significant pool of followers. Create Instagram and TikTok accounts as vehicles for building your pool of followers. There are some tricks to gaining followers such as posting interesting things that you think are likely to be reposted. The simplest approach, however, is to follow people in the hope that they will reciprocate, i.e., follow and interact with you.

If you are successful as an influencer, you might be able to charge for sponsored posts, create your own online store in which you sell products, add affiliate URLs in your bio, sell your photos, sell ads on your own podcast, make and sell merchandise, get paid to appear at events and more.

But even if you never use your following to promote a good or service made by someone else, you can use your "platform" to market your own goods and services.

F. CREATE AN ONLINE COURSE OR BECOME A TUTOR

If you enjoy being an educator, there are two good options for you.

• Create an online course: Producing and selling courses is one of the best ways to make money online. If you're an expert on a niche subject, it might be possible to monetize your expertise by generating courses on the Internet.

You can sell your course to an online educating site like Udemy or through your own website if you already have an established audience. Some course developers earn as much as $5,000 per month with their online courses.

Another way to sell educational materials is to use software like Adobe InDesign to create a learning book that has audio and video tracks embedded into the textbook that you create. According to a CNBC article dated February 6, 2023, a 35-year-old mom is bringing in $240,000 per month from selling a photography course online which consists of a teaching book with video embedded within it. It might be that people prefer this way to learn this way rather than with a standard Udemy style course.

You can fine-tune your offerings by looking at the reviews of similar courses. Find out what works and what does not work. If you have something to offer that will distinguish your course from the others, then highlight that as a selling point in your marketing.

• Become an online tutor: Having a teaching degree from your country of origin might be a fast track to getting tutoring gigs online.

While sciences and mathematics are typically the subjects in greatest demand for tutors, you'll also find teaching English as a second language (ESL) popular among international audiences.

A note on ESL gigs: Recently, a large number of Americans in Mexico made their living by teaching English to Chinese students remotely. Unfortunately, the Chinese government banned its citizens from learning English in this manner forcing Americans to pack up and leave Mexico due to the loss of their lucrative income stream.

This development in China makes teaching English as a second language (ASL) not as viable an option as it used to be. Despite this, there might still be a way to make some money teaching English online to students that are not Chinese nationals. You might find online tutoring jobs on websites such as Cambly, Preply, Tutor Me, Chegg Tutors, Tutor.com and Yup.

If you are a little rusty on a particular subject, you can refresh your memory by checking out Khan Academy which offers free online classes on a wide range of subjects: www.khanacademy.org.

G. PUBLISH AN E-BOOK

It has never been easier to publish an e-book with Amazon Kindle Direct Publishing. And since your agreement with Amazon isn't exclusive, you can also publish your e-book with Draft2Digital to expand your reach beyond Amazon's customer base.

You simply need to write the e-book, format it, create an e-book cover, publish it, and promote it. There are tools online to help you do those things, or you can even pay people to do those things for you. In fact, you could even hire a writer for your e-book, a graphic designer to design the cover, and a manuscript editor to eliminate errors from the content.

When developing the title of your e-book, look at the keywords in popular searches on Amazon. You can try the Keyword Tool to get a better idea of trending search words.

To generate sales for your e-book, there are tried and true marketing tricks that may generate excitement and buzz. For example, you can give the first few copies of your book away for free. Two other tricks are using paid influencers and video campaigns.

If you want to be a writer, it's recommended that you build a pool of followers using social media and blogs. This is known in the industry as having a "platform." Basically, when you announce your published book, your platform becomes a built-in marketing machine.

H. BECOME A GHOSTWRITER, EDITOR, TYPESETTER, PHOTO EDITOR AND MORE

Did you know that Fivver has a premium version of their freelance marketplace? You can find it at www.fiverr.com/pro and get started offering higher quality services for more money. You can also offer book writing/editing/typesetting services at Reedsy, Upwork, Guru or Freelancer.

There are so many services you can offer related to publishing: You can proofread. You can create an index for a nonfiction book. You can design a book cover.

If books are your passion, then this can be a great and fun source of income. You can develop skills by watching tutorials on YouTube and taking classes on relevant subjects at www.Udemy.com.

Nowadays, you can ghostwrite a book and get a little assistance from OpenAI's ChatGPT along the way. The key is that you are coming up with prompts for ChatGPT and then editing what ChatGPT comes up with. That makes it your own product. If you are writing a work of fiction, you can even ask ChatGPT to come up with backstories for your characters, and then you can work those backstories into your narrative.

I. START A BLOG

Finding a niche subject that is underserved can be a great starting point to a successful blog. You can make money from your blog using:

• Affiliate marketing, i.e., if you enroll in an affiliate marketing program, a business pays you money every time one of your readers clicks on a link and makes a qualifying purchase

• Placing ads in just the right places

• Selling physical or digital items directly from your own "shop"

• Writing a blog for an advertiser on a "sponsored by" basis

• Setting up a blog on Substack.com in order to get your readers to create direct revenue streams

• You can use the notoriety you have created about yourself to get work as a lecturer, endorser, presenter, media deals, etc.

J. CREATE AN APP

Even if you cannot create an app on your own, if you can come up with a good idea, then you can simply hire an app developer to build an app for you.

If you have the cash to pay for it, you can find a developer on a site like toptal.com.

Unfortunately, the operating system for Android phones and the operating system for iPhones (called IOS) are not compatible requiring separate sets of development.

You will have to decide if you want to first develop an app for an Android environment or first develop an app for an iPhone IOS. If you plan to generate revenue through advertisements and in-app purchases, then you should build on Android first. If, on the other hand, you are planning to generate revenue primarily by simply charging for each download of the App, then you should opt to build an app in iPhone IOS first.

K. BECOME A WRITER AND/OR EDITOR OF WEB CONTENT

One of the ways that companies are trying to differentiate themselves from their competitors is to fill their websites with content. This means that many companies are trying to hire writers for writers.

Try to identify a niche subject, like the travel and living experiences you have accumulated and wish to share. Yes, you can become an expert in your own corner of the world. Then get creative by putting your own twist/perspective into your articles. That way, you can differentiate your "voice" from all the others.

You might be able to find writing gigs via a website such as Craigslist, Media Bistro, Blogging Pro, Freelance Writing, Problogger or Flex Jobs.

L. BECOME A CODER, PROGRAMMER, DEVELOPER OR DATA SCIENTIST

Develop skills as a web designer/developer or enhance the skills you already have. For instance, you can take a complete course on web development at Udemy for less than $100. If you have an aptitude for logic and programming and you fully immerse yourself in the class, you could make a good living working remotely as a developer. Here is a link:

https://www.udemy.com/course/the-web-developer-bootcamp/

M. INVEST IN STOCKS, BONDS AND EXCHANGE-TRADED FUNDS (ETFS)

You can also make money by investing in stocks, bonds and exchange-traded funds (ETFs). ETFs are essentially "bundles" of stocks or bonds rather than just one single stock or one single bond. While day-trading has been shown to typically be a losing strategy for most people, purchasing and then holding investments over longer periods of time has been demonstrated as an effective means of attaining and increasing wealth. We should note that active trading or "day trading" is highly risky and rarely produces good results over time.

A great resource for understanding the evidence-based science of investing is the Common Sense Investing channel on YouTube with host Ben Felix: www.youtube.com/c/BenFelixCSI

N. SELL YOUR PHOTOGRAPHY AND/OR VIDEOS

Create an account with a website such as Alamy or Shutterstock or smartphone app Foap (Foap also lets you sell videos) and then upload your pictures and/or videos. Whenever someone downloads a copy of your image, you will get a royalty. Foap splits the profits with you 50/50.

O. BUY AND SELL DOMAIN NAMES

If you own a short, catchy, one-word .com domain, you might be able to find a buyer. You might also be able to sell a domain that contains one or more words that receive a high volume of searches.

Do some research at GoDaddy's Domain Auction to discover the types of names that receive the highest bids. It will give you some insight into what domains you should choose and whether or not there is a market for the domains you already own.

Be careful with domains that have a super trendy word in them. A domain you might be able to sell when a certain word is trending might sell for a lot less or not at all when the trend has lost its cachet.

You have two options as to how to go about selling a domain name: (a) you can simply post a web page offering to sell the domain at the domain's internet address a/k/a URL or (b) you can submit the domain name to a domain marketplace, such as GoDaddy's Domain Auction or Afternic.

P. REVIEW APPS AND WEBSITES

A site like UserTesting pays reviewers $10 to give other entrepreneurs feedback on their websites and apps. You'll be given a set of questions that you need to answer as you browse through a site.

You will then convey your ideas and feedback to the owners of the website or app via a video as you wade through their app or website. Let us say that your video is exactly 20 minutes long. If you do three videos per hour, you'll make $30.

It's that fast and easy. But there is competition so be sure to jump on each opportunity if it looks like something you prefer.

Q. BECOME A LIFE COACH

Here are some facts about life coaching: The life coaching industry in the United States is expected to bring in over $1 billion in revenue this year. There are over 18,000 life coaches in the U.S. alone.

Life coaching is about helping people gain insight into the obstacles that crop up in their lives, aiding them with developing motivation to tackle the challenges in their lives and helping them to identify any source of self-sabotage that might be undermining their efforts.

"Life coach" is a broad term that might consist of traditional style therapy, but also, business coaches, executive coaches, leadership coaches, dating coaches, relationship coaches, intimacy coaches and health coaches. Some package two or more subject areas into a bundle. It is important to not market yourself as a "psychologist," "psychotherapist," or "psychiatrist" unless you are actually licensed.

Below is a list of possible "platforms" that you can use to interact with clients and perform billing and other "housekeeping" tasks. Make sure you find out what the fee is (and do some comparison shopping) before you sign up for any of the following:

- Quenza.com
- Paperbell.com
- Delenta.com
- CoachAccountable.com
- Coaching Loft.com
- NudgeCoach.com

One kind of life coaching that has been picking up steam is sleep coaching. You can become a certified sleep coach and then do virtual consultations with people from all over the world.

R. BECOME A TIKTOK OR REEL CONSULTANT

One of the fastest growing gigs online is to market your services as a consultant on producing viral content on the TikTok or Instagram or Facebook platforms.

A video on Tiktok or a reel on Facebook or Instagram that goes viral has a huge potential and companies are starting to see the value in hiring a consultant. The beautiful thing is that you can act as a kind of broker.

Even if you do not personally have the ability to create a winning video, you can reach out to the young people who have a knack for it and hire them on behalf of the businesses that want to access the reach of TikTok or reels.

S. BECOME A VIDEO GAME COACH

Once you have a ranking as a top player in a certain video game, you can hold your hat out to others that want to become better players and coach them as they play. One such coach featured on cnbc.com claims that he started out streaming content on Twitch for free, but now coaches about 20 students per week, and he charges about $300 for a 90-minute session. He also charges a 20% royalty fee for any other coach that wants to be listed on his website. He currently has 6 such coaches listed on his website. He also earns revenue by streaming his coaching sessions on Facebook and posting educational videos to his YouTube channel and subscription-only Facebook group. He claims to be making $66,000 per month.

T. START DROPSHIPPING

With a dropshipping business, you create a storefront on the Internet, and then let a third-party deal with maintaining an inventory and then shipping goods to your buyers. It is not a complete walk in the park. You have to deal with setting prices, marketing, customer service, exchanges, refunds, etc.

One way to fulfill your orders is to have a shipment of your inventory shipped to Amazon and then let Amazon fulfill your orders using their "Fulfillment By Amazon" (FBA) program.

Most entrepreneurs have been focusing on the following marketing strategies: running Facebook ads, having influencers promote their products, developing a large following on social media and then telling your followers about your store.

U. VOICEOVER WORK

"In a world gone … to the golden voices?" There is a fairly large market for voiceover work, in part because of all the phone systems that have prerecorded messages. You can find voiceover work on Voices.com, Voices123, VoiceBunny and Fiverr.com. You can start out with a minimal investment, but if you find there is a market for your voice and you enjoy the work, you may want to up your voiceover game by purchasing a top-of-the-line microphone such as Rode NT USB mic, which costs about $170.

Then, you may want to get some kind of soundproofing to isolate the sound of your voice. Keep in mind that some of the following options are much more expensive than others: https://soundproofguide.com/8-best-soundproof-booth-for-voice-recording/.

Next, you can put it all together using a program called Audacity to edit your recordings in order to "distill" your finished product. Finally, you simply email your recording to the customer.

V. BECOME A CONSULTANT

People back in your country of origin or elsewhere in the world might want to hire you to use the skills and knowledge developed while you were still in your country of origin to help advise them. You can also develop new, possibly more saleable skills that you can then use as a consultant.

W. BECOME A MEDICAL DETECTIVE

Solve medical mysteries by signing up with CrowdMed. You don't have to be a doctor or even a medical professional to become a medical detective, and there are hundreds of active cases at any given time. The more successful you are in cracking cases, the more your reputation will grow and the more money you'll earn. During one of its fundraising runs, CrowdMed said the average detective earns $400 per solved case.

X. BECOME A "VIRTUAL ASSISTANT"

"Virtual Assistant" is becoming a popular new job, and it can pay as much as $100 per hour. For example, it might involve taking dictation, scheduling appointments, making phone calls, arranging travel, maintaining a social media presence or organizing emails.

You can find relevant job opportunities on websites like Upwork, Virtual Office Temps and/or Indeed.com. Be proactive and send emails to companies, executives and entrepreneurs, and see if they might like your help in running their businesses. This could be a great way to learn more about an industry that you are interested in.

Y. GET INTO MARKETING

• If you are good with words, you should consider becoming a copywriter. You can put yourself out there on a site like Fivver or you can search on job sites for a "freelance copywriter."

Nowadays, you can do copywriting and get a little assistance from OpenAI's ChatGPT along the way. The key is that you are coming up with prompts for ChatGPT and then editing what ChatGPT comes up with. That makes it your own product.

• Social media marketing: Most companies have a social media presence on sites like Facebook, Twitter, and Instagram. They hire people to market products and services, engage with existing customers and reach new ones.

• Email marketing: Remote email teams use collaborative design software to build successful email campaigns.

• Lead generation: This is the process of generating consumer interest for a product or service with the goal of turning that interest into a sale. In online marketing, this typically involves creating a popular website and then collecting visitors' contact information (called a "lead") via a web form. This contact information can then be sold to a company that will use it in their sales and marketing department. The key to this is to provide consumers with transparency and getting their informed consent before selling their information.

- Search engine optimization (SEO): Experts on Upwork offering SEO services charge as much as $125 per hour. Here's what SEO is, exactly, and how to get started.

How does one become an expert in SEO? There are various courses and certifications available online, including from search engines like Google itself. Colleges and universities offer courses as well. These range from free to as much as $1,000 each, so do your research before signing up to make sure you're taking the best course for you.

Once you've learned the basics, the best way to build that knowledge base is by getting some on-the-ground experience. Create profiles on sites like Fiverr and Upwork and start picking up gigs on sites like ZipRecruiter, LinkedIn and Monster. The more experience you accrue, the more valuable you'll become as an expert and the more you'll ultimately be able to charge.

As long as search engines are a key way in which people find what they're looking for, the skill likely won't go away. "You spend all this time and all this money building your site," says Lilani of companies' attitudes, "if nobody can find it, again, why did you do that?"

Search engine optimization is the process of ensuring your website gets picked up in organic searches, say, if someone is looking for the kind of products you sell or the kind of content you cover. Imagine doing a search for French fries, snowboarding or Donna Summer on Google. SEO helps sites show up closer to the top of the list Google shows you that aren't ads.

Experts in search engines like Google and Bing study tactics to ensure the platform considers your site a go-to on whatever you're offering. They'll make sure it includes relevant keywords, links and content, among other tactics.

"Search engine optimization is paramount if you want to be found when people are doing online searches," says Yolanda Owens, career expert at The Muse, adding that it's "increasingly becoming more and more valuable." And employers are on the hunt for experts in the field.

A search for SEO jobs on ZipRecruiter results in more than 14,000 open roles, both part-time and full-time.

Z. WORK YOUR CURRENT JOB REMOTELY

If you are currently employed, talk to your employer about working remotely. And then do your job from outside the United States.

NOTE: If your employer is in the United States, then you will likely want to make sure that they continue to treat you as a resident of the United States for tax purposes. If you are a taxpayer in any other country, you will want to confer with tax professionals in that country before doing anything that might affect your current tax resident status.

WORK ANY JOB THAT CAN BE DONE REMOTELY

Think about all the jobs you may have had in the past: perhaps you have been a designer, teacher, newspaper editor, translator, etc., and then think about the possibility of doing that job remotely. Check a website like Indeed.com and find out if there are any positions available for doing that work remotely.

Or, think about doing any other sort of job remotely even if you have no direct experience in it. You can find ideas on Indeed.com and LinkedIn. Talk to recruiters and find out what skills they are looking for. If needed, develop those skills.

Obviously, certain jobs cannot be done remotely. You can collect operate on someone's glaucoma remotely, for instance. But a surprising number of jobs can be done remotely.

You can also research remote work at regular job recruitment sites. Additionally, you can find freelance work on sites such as Fiverr, Upwork, Freelancer and many others.

Build a portfolio that demonstrates your competence even if it means doing mock-ups for free. You might even need to offer your services for free or a low price to get your start and build up reviews and customers. Freelancing may require an increased effort to individualize your communications with clients in order to set yourself apart from the pack.

AFFORDING COUNTRY X AS A RETIREE

Most people afford their retirement abroad by drawing on Social Security-style programs, private annuities, pensions, tax-advantaged retirement accounts and taxable brokerage accounts. These are probably the major financial avenues in which most people fund their new life adventure in Country X. Others choose to finance their life in Country X by selling or renting out their home in their country of origin. Still others find creative ways to bring in supplemental income.

We'll discuss some of the ways to supplement your income below, and also in a special book on the subject to be released shortly. But first, let us talk about how U.S. residents or citizens may be able to maximize their Social Security benefits. If you are not a resident or citizen of the United States, this section on Social Security benefits may not apply to you.

Whether you are a U.S. citizen or not, we urge you to speak with an expert in your country of origin about how to maximize your Social Security or public pension benefits in your home country.

• Maxime Your Social Security (U.S.)

In the United States, Social Security benefits accounts for, on average, 33% of a retiree's total income, and it may count for even more if your income level is lower than average.

• Earn Income Prior to Retirement

Social Security calculates what is referred to as your average indexed monthly earnings for the 35 years in which you earned the most. Social Security applies a formula to those earnings and arrives at your basic benefit, or primary insurance amount (PIA). Your PIA is the amount you would receive at your full retirement age (FRA), which is 65 or older, depending on your date of birth.

The key to increasing your monthly benefit, therefore, is to replace the low-income years that are included in the 35-year calculation with higher-income years.

Social Security rewards higher lifetime average earnings. Increase your earnings per year and/or increase the years you work in order to maximize your PIA.

"Should I delay benefits for a bigger payout?"

Social Security retirement benefits are increased by a certain percentage (depending on your date of birth) if you delay your retirement beyond full retirement age or FRA.

A significant thing to note about the advantage of delaying is that the benefit increase disappears when you reach age 70, even if you continue to delay taking benefits. NOTE: There is no advantage in delaying from age 70 and above.

The later you start your Social Security (up to age 70), the more you'll get per month. And if you live to at least average life expectancy, you'll get a higher lifetime payout too.

Social Security refers to this as delayed retirement credits or DRC.

While delaying retirement may increase your overall benefits, especially if you live your full, expected lifespan or more, you need to weigh the benefit you get by delaying your benefits against the time value of money.

The time value of money essentially means that a sum of money in hand today has greater value than the same sum to be paid in the future.

For one thing, if you are able to invest the Social Security money you receive and produce a rate of return that is greater than what you will receive by delaying your Social Security benefit, then you might actually be better off by NOT delaying.

In addition to considering the time value of money, you must factor in your expected life expectancy. If you live a shorter life than most, you might receive far less, in the aggregate, if you delay taking benefits.

For example, someone who delays taking Social Security benefits until they reach age 67 and then dies at age 68 will likely receive far less in total benefits than someone who started their Social Security benefits at age 62 and then dies at age 68.

This is true even if the person who took their Social Security benefits at 62 was receiving far less per month than the person who delayed taking their Social Security benefits until age 67.

A. Use an Online Calculator

Consider using any number of software programs and online calculators to model how best to maximize your Social Security benefit.

There are so many moving parts in the Social Security filing process that it can be very confusing. For instance, a married couple both turning 62, has 81 different age combinations to consider. Software can show which variables play the biggest role in determining the payout numbers.

B. Determine Your Life Expectancy

This can be a risky calculation because there are so many variables. Longevity can be a key factor in calculating when to claim Social Security. If you have parents and other relatives that have lived a long lifetime plus if you are healthy, and you have a healthful lifestyle, then postponing might make more sense for you than it would for others.

Conversely, if your family members tend to not live very long past the age of 65 or if you are not very healthy or have a lot of risk factors, then delaying might not make a lot of sense.

C. Consider Undoing Your Social Security Benefits

Social Security allows you to "rewind" your original application for retirement benefits within the 12 months of the date you first claimed your benefits.

You have to repay all the money you received but then you can restart your Social Security, right then or later, and get more per month. This might be a great option if you come into some money, like a big inheritance, after your Social Security starts.

You would start the process by completing Social Security form SSA-521.

NOTE: If you miss a filing date window, you are allowed a six-month lookback.

D. Consider Suspending Payments

Anyone from FRA to 70 can voluntarily suspend their own Social Security payments for any number of months, up to age 70. When payments resume, they will be higher.

NOTE: Suspending your own payments could also stop any spousal or child payments on your record, which might be disastrous for you and your family.

E. Consider Restricting Your Social Security Application

One interesting way to optimize your Social Security benefits is called restricted application.

If you or your spouse were born on or before Jan. 1, 1954, this idea might work for you. People in this category may be able to collect a spousal benefit based on their spouse's earnings record, thereby delaying your own individual benefit and allowing it to continue to grow.

F. Consider Coordinating Your Benefits

You might be eligible for two or more kinds of Social Security payments. Included among them, your own, spousal, survivors, widow's or more.

By coordinating and timing your various benefits you can substantially increase your lifetime payout. While this might be a bit tricky, there are online services that can provide guidance to help you make your decisions.

When married couples file, they need to look at their combined benefits. We recommend that you consider making decisions as a team and not as individuals. The timing as to when each person files can substantially affect the total payout that the couple receives.

The total picture: Whenever you make decisions about when to file for your benefits, make sure that you take into account your complete financial and economic holdings, including your other sources of income such as pensions and IRAs. Consequently, you will also need to consider the tax liability of any actions you might take.

LOCATE EACH OLD 401(k) (U.S.)

You might be surprised to learn that billions of dollars of 401(k) assets have gone unclaimed in the United States. Make sure that you have lined up your 401(k)-type assets from all your prior employers to help fund your retirement.

The following are some steps you can take if you think some funds might be missing:

1. Contact Your Former Employer

The first place you should look is your prior employer. Contact their human resources department if they have one. They should have all of the information as to the whereabouts of the 401(k) account you had with them.

Request that they send you the proper paperwork and help you facilitate the transfer of your funds to whatever account you choose.

If they are unable to locate any information on your account, they should be able to provide you with the contact information of the "plan administrator" who handled your 401(k) on their behalf.

Let the administrator know your situation, and just like the HR department, they should be able to assist you in moving your money properly.

2. Locate Your Old 401(K) Statements

If you are having difficulty reaching your former employer's HR department, refer to an account statement of your old 401(k) instead.

If you are still living at the same address, you may be receiving yearly or quarterly statements in the mail. Check your statement for information on where your account is held and any contact information.

The information on your statements will come in handy in identifying how much money you may be able to transfer over to make sure nothing is left behind.

3. Search Unclaimed Assets Databases

If your search isn't producing results, for example, your former employer has gone out of business or the enterprise was bought by another company, you may still be able to retrieve your assets.

It may take a little more effort and research but there are many national databases that can help you track down your old 401(k) accounts.

4. Find 401(k)s with your Social Security Number

All your 401(k)s are linked to your social security number when you enrolled. Theoretically, you should be able to find all your 401(k)s using only your SSN. In practice, however, it may be difficult for you to do so on your own.

Resources to Help You Conduct Your Search

• The Department of Labor's Abandoned Plan database can help you identify what happened to your old plan and provide you with the contact information of the current administrator.

• The National Registry of Unclaimed Retirement Benefits may allow you to do a free search for any unclaimed retirement money using just your Social Security number.

• FreeERISA is another free resource that will help you search for any old account information that has been filed with the federal government.

• The Securities and Exchange Commission's website or your state's Secretary of State can provide more information on your previous employer.

Conclusion: If you think you might need some help corralling together your old 401(k)s, consider using a company like Beagle (www.MeetBeagle.com) to conduct a comprehensive 401(k) search using your SSN. Once they find your 401(k)s, they also help you with the tedious rollover process. Make sure that you consult with competent financial and tax experts about the best way to transfer your 401(k) account(s) into another kind of account and what kind of account will best suit your needs.

TIMING YOUR TRANSFERS OF MONEY TO COUNTRY X

The ideal times to transfer money to Country X are those times when the currency in the country where your money is sitting is unusually strong against the local currency. To check on the exchange rate for the U.S. dollar, for example, simply visit google.com and type: '1 usd to [name of local currency] to get the current exchange rate. Then click on '1Y' to see how the U.S. dollar has performed against, say, the Mexican peso for the past 12 months. If the graph is moving upwards and the U.S. dollar is stronger than it has been recently, that might indicate that it's a good time to transfer a portion of your money from a U.S. account into a Country X account.

You can check the exchange rate every few days to see how the value of the currency you hold, such as the US dollar, is trending relative to the local currency.

An upward spike occurs when the number of pesos needed to equal 1 US dollar has increased.

Example: All of a sudden, instead of 19 pesos being needed to equal to 1 US dollar, 24 Mexican pesos are suddenly needed to equal 1 US dollar. This shows an increased strength in the U.S. dollar against the Mexican peso. Thus, when you see an upward spike that means that the US dollar is growing stronger against the peso, and it may be advantageous to transfer money from your bank account or your investment account in your country of origin to your Country X bank account. This is especially true when the dollar is stronger against the peso than it has been in months or years.

As a disclaimer, the amount of money that you transfer is based on your own speculation about how the exchange rate will trend in the future and on the amount of money that you will need to have in order to fund your lifestyle in Country X. We are not telling you in this book when to transfer foreign currency to your Country X bank account. Deciding when to transfer funds is a judgment call for you to make with the counsel of your professional advisers.

Also, for the sake of clarification, any transfer of dollars from one of your accounts in one financial institution to a different currency in another of your accounts in another financial institution should not be characterized or conceptualized as either a "transaction on a foreign exchange market" or a "transaction in a futures market." Those are totally different things than what we are talking about. We are simply discussing real-time conversion of actual money from one currency to another by transferring money from an account in a banking institution in one country to an account in another banking institution in Country X (even if both banks are owned by the same company).

If, for example, you decide it is advantageous to make an all-cash home purchase in Country X by transferring money from an account in your country of origin to a bank account in Country X, you might want to wait for an upward spike in the chart, and simply rent a home on a monthly basis until the dollar gets stronger before you convert your dollars (or any other currency) into the local currency.

NOTE: We are not necessarily recommending that you purchase a home in Country X. We are simply using this as an example showing how to time major purchases. It could save you thousands of dollars over the years if you time things just right.

INCOME STREAMS IN THE COUNTRY WHERE YOU ARE LIVING

> **Important Note**
>
> If you are currently a U.S. taxpayer, make sure that earning money in Country X is the most advantageous strategy available to you before you seek out sources of income in Country X. We say this in light of the possible tax savings you might benefit from due to the Foreign Earned Income Exclusion (FEIE) discussed in Chapter 14. It might be that finding income sources outside of Country X will yield the best net results.

Keep in mind that, when you seek out sources of income in Country X you may need a work permit. This is especially true if you are not a citizen of Country X or given an automatic pass to earn income in Country X. Check with your team of legal experts in Country X to find out if you do need a work permit.

Also, you will need to determine if you will owe taxes to the United States or to Country X. In order to make this determination, you should speak to a team of competent team of legal and tax professionals both in the U.S. and in Country X to make sure you are paying tax to the correct country and to make sure that you are reporting your income and taxes paid to the right countries even if you are not paying taxes to every country.

Here are some of the ways you might be able to earn income from sources in Country X:

• Offering services to other expats: While you may not be able to earn the same kind of money that you earned doing what you did for a living in your country of origin, expats may be willing to pay you more than you would otherwise make in Country X because they may prefer to do business with someone who speaks their language and was trained in the country of their own origin or a country that is similar to the country of their own origin.

- Be a real estate agent.
- Be a travel guide.
- Be an AirBnB or VRBO host (or manage the AirBnBs or VRBOs of other owners).
- Be a private driver for expats. For example, you could be hired full-time or on an à la carte basis, such as on runs to and from the airport.
- Be a private chef.
- Work for the embassy of your country of origin: Embassies and consulates tend to have work available for their citizens living abroad.
- Get jobs at a hotel or resorts: You do not necessarily have to be fluent in more than one language but it helps: https://www.transitionsabroad.com/listings/work/shortterm/tourism_hospitality_gap_year_jobs_abroad.shtml
- Become a wedding officiant/event planner/photographer. Many people from around the world travel to Country X for a "destination wedding." Why not provide services to them?
- There are also opportunities to find work in exchange for room and board, such as through worldpackers.com: https://www.worldpackers.com/search/work_exchange/
- Another possibility is to house sit (which often includes pet sitting) for people when they are away from their homes in Country X.

• You may also find work teaching English as a second language in person to citizens of Country X. You may need to have a college degree and be certified to teach ESL.

• Seek out a conventional job in Country X at a job portal.

☆ ☆ ☆ ☆ ☆

For more resources and additional information to help you start an exciting new chapter in your life, please visit our website at www.AllPointsGuide.com.

10. RISKS POSED BY PEOPLE

IN THIS CHAPTER, we deal with the risks posed by other human beings that you may encounter while living abroad.

VIOLENT CRIME

Most of the violent crime in the world is related to narcotics trafficking. It is very rare that foreign nationals, who are not involved in narcotics trafficking, other kinds of crime, politics and journalism are targeted with violent crime. If you can avoid being involved in narcotics trafficking and also avoid the neighborhoods, towns, cities and regions where such violent crime is occurring, your chances of being the victim of a violent crime will be drastically reduced. This is true of any country.

Before visiting or residing in a particular country (that we shall refer to as Country X), always check the U.S. State Department's travel advisories to Country X before taking any trip to or within Country X.

KIDNAPPING

The chance that you will be kidnapped in Country X is probably very low. We do, however, have some tips for you if you want to further reduce the chance of being kidnapped.

HOW TO AVOID BEING KIDNAPPED

Despite the recent uptick of foreigners being targeted, you can still reduce your chance of being kidnapped by sticking to the following rules:

1. Do NOT get inside any unmarked taxis.

2. Choose Uber or DiDi over marked taxis. Make sure to verify that the license plate of the vehicle matches the license plate identified by Uber or DiDi and that the driver's face and name match the photo and name supplied by Uber or DiDi. Ask him what his name is. Don't ask, "Is your name 'Juan?'" You need to test him to make sure he gives the right name. Ask, "What is your name?" or "*Como se llama usted?*"

3. If you get into any car that you do not own, check to make sure that there is a handle on the inside of the door that works. Do not enter any vehicle without making sure that the handle inside the door works by seeing if the latching mechanism on the side of the door moves when you squeeze the handle.

When pulling the handle inside the car door you should see the safety latch move. The arrow points at this mechanism.

4. You should also make sure that the child safety lock key is in the "off" position. If it is in the "on" position, or if the door handle inside the vehicle is not working, do not get into the vehicle. Take a ride with someone else.

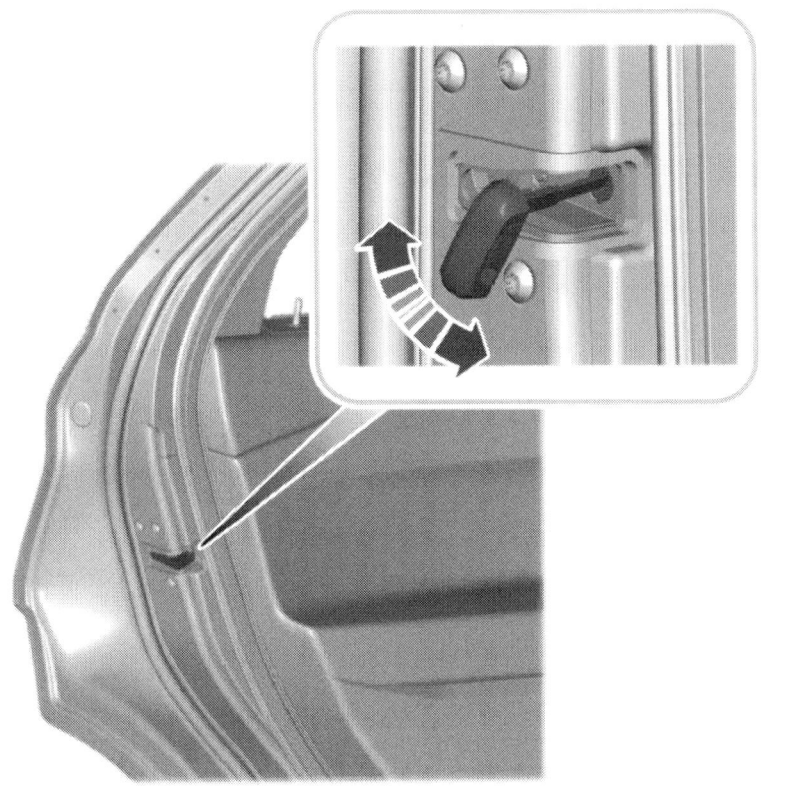

If the child safety lock has been locked, or if the handle is not working from inside the vehicle, do NOT enter the vehicle

5. Do your own driving. This is probably the safest way to travel.

6. Do not drive around Country X in a flashy car or display great wealth in other ways like wearing expensive watches or jewelry.

7. Do not drive at night, either as a passenger or driver.

8. Take toll roads whenever possible.

9. Do not work for a large company with deep pockets that operates in Country X, such as a factory that makes cars for an international automaker. If you do, would-be kidnappers might kidnap you because they think that your company will pay a handsome reward for your safe return.

10. Live in a city or region where many people are affluent, or at least, where there is a large, solid middle class. If you are the only person around that has a good supply of money, then you may unknowingly be presenting yourself as a target.

11. Avoid the places and regions that the U.S. State Department tells you to avoid.

12. Do not get involved in narcotics trafficking or any other illegal activity while you are in Country X.

If you follow the above rules, the chances of you being kidnapped will drop dramatically. But do keep in mind that the chance of anyone (especially a tourist or nomad or expat) being kidnapped is extremely remote.

"If I cannot avoid being kidnapped, what can I do to increase the chances of getting found or released?"

There are four main ways to increase the chance that you will be rescued in the event that you are kidnapped. All of them require you to take preventive steps before the kidnapping occurs. The **first way** is to purchase kidnapping insurance prior to your trip. The **second way** is to take a snapshot of the license plate of the car you are getting into and text it to people you can count on to contact the authorities on your behalf. The **third way** to ensure your safe return is to share your GPS coordinates with a trusted person when you are traveling. The **fourth way** is to get on the phone with someone you trust while you are being driven by someone you don't know.

Sharing GPS Coordinates and Getting on the Phone

You can easily share your GPS coordinates by opening up Google Maps on your phone, clicking on your photo icon and then clicking on "location sharing." Once you have selected someone, call the person you trust on the phone and have a chat with them during the drive.

If your driver starts acting or driving suspiciously, you can communicate that information to the person on the phone. Then, if you report that you are being kidnapped, they can contact the authorities and tell them exactly what your last known location is right away. They can also share the license plate of the vehicle.

SAFETY TIPS FOR WOMEN TRAVELERS

Women can travel in many countries in relative safety. We recommend that you increase your level of safety by following these rules:

1. Travel with at least one other person, when possible, and try to avoid traveling at night.

2. Be careful when you drink in bars and nightclubs, refusing any drink handed to you by someone other than the bartender. Sticking to water in bars is probably your best bet because water's absence of flavor might enable you to taste any adulterations.

3. Avoid walking around with your cellphone in your hand.

4. Wear sunglasses, when possible and safe to do so, in order to avoid making eye contact with strangers.

AGGRESSIVE SALESPEOPLE
(SELLING TIMESHARE AND PRE-CONSTRUCTION HOMES)

Until you have been coerced, tricked or bribed into attending a timeshare meeting, you really have no idea just how overwhelming the experience can be. It is almost like a cult induction, and people often end up signing away a big chunk of their life savings to purchase a profoundly bad investment that isn't worth nearly what they paid for it and comes with maintenance costs that will continue to increase the net cost.

At the meeting, the true initial and maintenance costs of the package will likely be hidden from you, and you will NOT be told how difficult it will be to sell or simply terminate your timeshare package if you decide you no longer want it.

If someone you do not know approaches you about a time share or a free seminar about real estate or offers you a free meal or entertainment, we urge you to avoid making eye contact and keep walking forward. Wearing sunglasses is a great aid if you want to avoid making eye contact.

For more information about just how bad an investment a timeshare truly is, read the entry on timeshares in Chapter 15.

NOTE: There are now people selling pre-construction homes as aggressively as timeshares have previously been sold. This is a relatively recent development. Selling pre-construction homes isn't necessarily a scam in and of itself, but using aggressive sales tactics is more than a bit predatory. Our recommendation is to avoid aggressive salespeople no matter what they are selling. In general, you are better off making decisions as a consumer when you are not under pressure.

THE "ELASTIC PRICING" SCAM

The most common scam that you will encounter is someone offering to sell you something and you agree. Neither of you, however, has mentioned or agreed to a price. Then, you take possession of that item and may even bite into it or start to drink from it and they tell you that you now owe them an extravagant amount of money that does not remotely keep in step with the value of what you have intended to purchase.

For instance, a kid might sell you a can of cold soda and then, once you take the first sip, tell you that you now owe them the equivalent of $20 USD. Another form of this scam happens in taxis: Once you arrive at the destination, they'll tell you that the 3-minute ride costs $100 USD.

This sort of scam can happen in many kinds of places, including street vendors, shops, restaurants, etc.

There are four ways to avoid this scam (which we like to call "The Elastic Pricing Scam"):

First, develop strong skills in the language most spoken in Country X. When someone knows that you speak their language well, they are less likely to think that they can get away with taking advantage of you.

Second, always, always, always ask for the price before making a purchase.

Third, carry around a small pad of paper and a pen and ask the seller to write down the amount in local currency prior to agreeing to the purchase. You should write down the word for the currency before or after they write in the number of pesos so that it's clear that the price that they quote you is in local currency and not U.S. dollars.

Fourth, if, after you make a purchase, you are given a receipt, then make sure to hold onto that receipt, do not lose it and keep it somewhere that will allow you to quickly retrieve it.

Two Reasons to Ask for the Price Before Agreeing to Purchase a Good or Service

In general, it is good to ask what things cost before you agree to a service or good, even if you are in, say, a hospital. It is in your best interest, however, to ask what things cost for two reasons:

A. There will be no "sticker shock" when you finally receive an invoice for services rendered.

B. Once you know what the price is, you can try to haggle or negotiate to see if you can lower the price.

Even a doctor or hospital might have a little "wiggle room" in their prices if you ask extremely diplomatically. You might even want to get a price quote from a second doctor and compare the two prices. The difference between the two might be staggering. And keep in mind that what might fly in the face of standard etiquette in your home country might be just fine in Country X.

Even in a country like the United States, more prices are open to negotiation than most people realize, but haggling is a much bigger part of the culture in other parts of the world, even when dealing with doctors and hospitals. The trick is being very diplomatic, respectful and subtle when you ask whether the price is negotiable.

THE "YOU OWE ME A HUGE TIP" SCAM

Taxicab drivers are known, albeit rarely, to tell you that you owe them an outrageous tip on top of the ride for which you just paid and received a receipt that you did not lose. Imagine that a taxi in New York City informed you after a five-minute ride that you are required to give them a $100 tip. It is hard to imagine that happening anywhere. But it can happen in rare instances in Country X.

How to Deal with the "You Owe Me a Huge Tip" Scam

There are two ways to deal with this scam:

1. Avoid taxis and, instead, use rideshare services like Uber or DiDi (or even going one step further by hiring your own private driver (either on a full-time or à la carte basis).

2. Have your camera ready and start video recording and broadcasting the interaction. Be sure to keep your camera out of reach. They will likely be so afraid of the consequences if you go to the authorities that they will immediately leave and let you go.

MISCELLANEOUS SCAMS

ATM Scams

One of the most common scams involving ATMs involves skimmers and cameras. These is a problem that can and does occur in every country of the world.

Skimmers are devices placed just outside the part where you place your debit card. As you slide your card inside, it reads and records the data inside the magnetic strip for later, fraudulent use. At the same time that the skimmer is illegally capturing the data encoded on your card's magnetic strip, there is typically a camera nearby that is video recording your fingers as you type in your PIN code.

"What do I do about these skimmers and cameras?"

First, avoid random ATMs you might see at a shop or convenience store and only use name-brand bank ATMs.

Second, look at the ATM to see if there is some extra hardware in front of where you put your card. If there is anything about it that looks suspicious, do not use it and report it to the bank.

Third, if you see no tell-tale signs of skimming, you may proceed but make sure that, as you type your PIN with your dominant hand, you use your other hand to cover up or shield what your dominant hand is typing. You can even pretend to touch the wrong buttons in order to further obfuscate what you are actually typing.

Criminals placed a "skimmer" just outside of where the card is inserted

Currency Conversion Scams

Just to be 100% accurate and fair, we should note that the exchange rate scams you are reading about in this section are not illegal at all. But from an ethical point of view, they may not stand up to scrutiny.

Conversion Rates at Restaurants or Stores

If, when you are paying with a credit card, you are ever asked at a restaurant or at any other place of business if you want to pay your bill in local currency or in U.S. dollars, always answer as follows: "the [local currency]." You want to pay in the local currency. Otherwise, your transaction could be subject to a much less favorable exchange rate.

An easy way to sidestep this dilemma is to simply carry the local currency around with you and pay with cash. Just make sure that, if you are paying by cash, you have a mix of denominations with you. If you are only carrying large bills, some establishments will not be able to accommodate you.

Ultimately, you may decide to open up a local bank account at a local bank and then pay for things with the debit card provided by your local bank. That way no conversion is necessary.

Conversion Rate at an ATM

Another time that exchange rate problems can crop up is when you are at an ATM. You should know that a common trick that banks try to pull is to offer you a service called Dynamic Currency Conversion (DCC). This is a conversion that is not done at the official exchange rate. If you opt for a DCC, then you would essentially be allowing the ATM conjure up its own exchange rate for you.

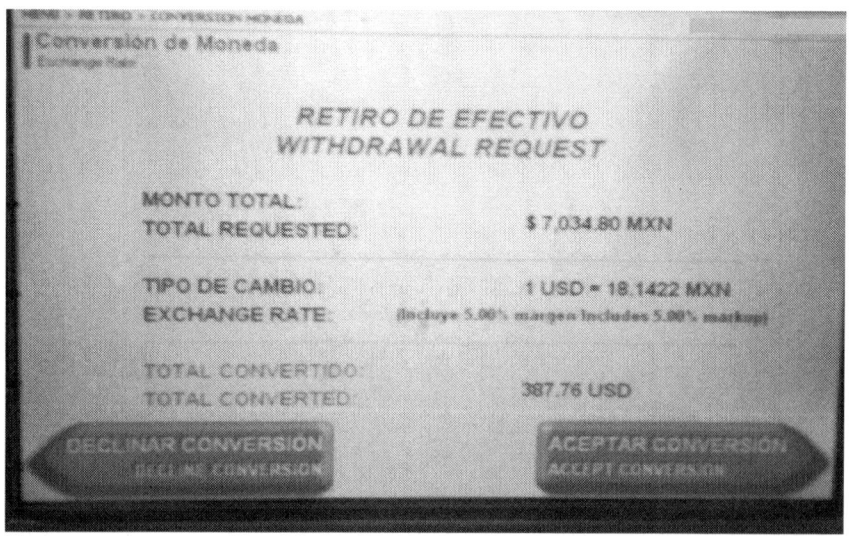

If you see a screen like this hit "DECLINE CONVERSION"

Not only is the exchange rate likely to be in the bank's favor, the DCC service often comes with fees that are not even disclosed. If you see an offer for Dynamic Currency Conversion (DCC) hit the "no" button.

Being Asked for Handouts by Neighbors

You may not consider yourself to be super rich, but there is a chance that your local neighbors in Country X will make that assumption simply because you are from the U.S. Unfortunately, this may lead some of your bolder neighbors to ask you for money, sometimes on many occasions as if they have never asked you and been turned down by you before.

For this reason, you may find that you prefer to live in a neighborhood that, by local standards, is solidly middle class or even somewhat more affluent. The housing costs may be somewhat higher there, but you will likely have more pleasant encounters with your neighbors.

Petty Theft

Just as you need to be mindful no matter where you are in the world, it is best to keep your belongings safe. When you are walking around Country X, it's best to not hold your cellphone in your hand as an invitation to have it easily stolen. You can secure your valuables by checking out travel catalogues that feature secure passports, wallets, clothing etc. Make sure that your wallet and other valuables are secure. You might consider wearing pants with hidden pockets and backpacks that have no access to the public.

Political Unrest

We recommend that you check the news to make sure there is political stability in a country before you try to live there.

☆ ☆ ☆ ☆ ☆

For more resources and additional information to help you start an exciting new chapter in your life, please visit our website at www.AllPointsGuide.com.

11. PUBLIC BENEFITS, LONG-TERM CARE & HEALTHCARE

PLANNING FOR YOUR FUTURE healthcare and long-term care needs is extremely important. In this chapter we will take you through some of the issues that you are most likely to face. Discussing your own unique situation with experts is highly advised.

If you're young, then the discussion on public benefits programs might be irrelevant for you at this point in your life and you can skip to the discussion on healthcare. If you are of retirement age, however, you will want to take a careful look at everything in this chapter so that these issues are starting to appear on your "radar screen" as you think about your future.

PUBLIC BENEFITS PROGRAMS

As we have discussed, we urge you to not revoke your current citizenship in the United States even if you become a citizen of Country X. The main reason for maintaining your citizenship is that you can minimize the possibility of being denied coverage at some point by whatever public or private insurance provider you are eligible for in your country of origin in case you ever need to return to your country of origin to receive care.

You should seriously consider returning home to your country of origin in the event that you require round-the-clock skilled nursing care. This level of intense care may not be available in the manner you desire in Country X. Alternatively, you may need to rely on a public benefits program in your country of origin for free or reduced cost coverage. Below are some selected programs in the United States for which you might want to maintain your eligibility.

U.S. Programs: Federally Administered Programs

The Social Security Administration administers Social Security benefits and Social Security Disability Insurance (SSDI). These aren't considered "needs-based" programs because they're not based on a beneficiary's financial need. Even if you are quite affluent, you might still be eligible to receive these benefits.

When you sign up for your Social Security benefit, make sure you enroll in their Representative Payee Program so that a trusted person you know can manage your benefits during a period of mental incapacity, and keep in mind that a period of mental incapacity may be permanent in some cases due to conditions such as Alzheimer's and other forms of dementia.

Centers for Medicare & Medicaid Services (CMS) is the federal government agency that administers Medicare. Medicare is the federal government program that provides healthcare coverage if you're one of the following: (1) age 65 and above, (2) under age 65 and receiving Social Security Disability Insurance (SSDI) for a certain amount of time, or (3) under 65 and with End-Stage Renal Disease (ESRD).

U.S. Programs: State Administered Programs

Supplement Security Income (SSI) is a needs-based program funded at the federal level and administered at the state level. It is more commonly referred to as "welfare." The beauty of SSI is that even if you are only eligibly for $1 of SSI you automatically qualify for Medicaid (or California's Medi-Cal). You can't receive SSI while in Country X, though.

Medicaid is a needs-based (financial needs) healthcare program. It can also cover in-patient lodging expenses for people in a skilled nursing facility (SNF) in the United States.

NOTE: In order to qualify for a needs-based program you cannot have excessive income or assets. The only exception to this is for Medicaid or MediCal in the context of paying for a skilled nursing facility, in which case there is no upper limit on income, but any income you receive, minus a small amount you can keep for incidentals, goes towards paying your nursing home bill each month.

Assisted living isn't the most intensive level of in-patient care you can receive. Patients that require greater care receive a higher level of care in skilled nursing facilities. If Country X does not have its own equivalent to the skilled nursing facilities found in the United States and elsewhere, you *may consider* (or the people caring for you might consider on your behalf) your RETURN TO THE UNITED STATES for the purpose of getting that higher level of care.

If you do not have privately funded long-term care coverage to pay for it, you and/or your loved ones will find that it can be quite expensive. More often than not, if you're from the United States, it makes sense to explore your eligibility for Medicaid (or Medi-Cal as it's known in California). Keep in mind that this is something you might be eligible for even if your income level is so high that it makes you ineligible for SSI.

If you are considering your admission to a skilled nursing facility, we recommend that you work with an elder law attorney to determine if you are eligible or, if not, what you would need to do to in order to become eligible.

A good source for finding an elder law attorney in the United States is the National Academy of Elder Law Attorneys (NAELA) website, but you need to do your own due diligence to make sure that any attorney you find is qualified.

Find an "elder law" attorney near you using an organization like NAELA: https://naela.org/findlawyer.

You will still need to vet whatever lawyers are practicing near you. NAELA does not do that for you. It simply is a repository of members that claim to be elder law attorneys without any certification process ensuring that they are qualified.

HEALTHCARE WHILE LIVING ABROAD

It is very important that you have a plan in place to deal with any health needs you might have while living in Country X. The mere fact that you are young and healthy is not a good reason to ignore having a health care plan in place because there are no guarantees that some catastrophic event won't happen to you, not even if you are super young and healthy.

Health Coverage for People Hopping from Country to Country

If you are a digital nomad or simply hopping from country to country, then we would recommend that you purchase traveler's insurance that covers emergent and medical evacuation needs. Some of the top-rated providers of this kind of coverage include HTH Worldwide, Seven Corners and IMG Global. If you have any preexisting conditions, consider Generali Global Assistance. If you have a dog, we recommend IMG.

Keep in mind that these kinds of plans might only cover emergency health care and/or medical evacuations while you are overseas. That kind of coverage will get you safely back home where you will receive healthcare coverage that is *not* covered by your traveler's insurance plan.

Thus, you will need to pair your travel insurance plan like with healthcare coverage back in the United States. You may have Medicare or Medicaid back in the United States, you might have healthcare coverage through your employer or you might have some kind of healthcare coverage through the Patient Protection and Affordable Care Act and colloquially known as Obamacare.

If you do not have any kind of coverage in the United States and you do not have full coverage overseas, then we recommend that you consider purchasing healthcare coverage through an Obamacare exchange. You can visit this site, and actually purchase insurance through it: https://www.healthcare.gov/marketplace-in-your-state/.

The Time to Enroll in Healthcare Programs

The right time to enroll for healthcare coverage in when you are YOUNG AND HEALTHY.

There might be public health care plans you can buy into. It is important you do when you are healthy, especially if they have limitations or restriction placed on foreigners with pre-existing conditions. Don't wait until you have a condition that will exclude you from coverage.

The same is true for long-term private coverage. If it fits in your budget, and it makes sense for you, then sign up right away for a plan from CIGNA Global, GeoBlue, William Russell or another insurance company offering private health insurance coverage in Country X. Do not wait until a health problem crops up because it could make you ineligible for coverage.

For People Living in One Country Long-term

If you are living in one country long-term, then we recommend that you research the kind of coverage available to you there. You might be able to "buy in" to a national, subsidized healthcare program. These types of program can often offer decent or better care at possibly sensational prices compared to the cost of coverage in the U.S. Alternatively, you can purchase International Private Medical Insurance (IPMI) discussed immediately below.

PRIVATE HEALTH INSURANCE

International Medical/Health Insurance (commonly known as International Private Medical Insurance or IPMI), is a type of policy that can cover your medical expenses while you are living abroad. Some of the major providers of IPMI include CIGNA Global, GeoBlue and William Russell. There are also other companies offering IPMI.

Important Note on Exclusions of Pre-Existing Conditions

CIGNA Global, GeoBlue, William Russell or another insurance company offering private health insurance coverage around the globe and other providers of private, international health insurance have the right to exclude coverage for pre-existing conditions. The Affordable Care Act in the United States that requires insurers to not deny coverage on the basis of a pre-existing condition does not apply in other countries.

If you are excluded from both IMSS and international private coverage like CIGNA Global, GeoBlue, William Russell, or another provider but you are enrolled in Medicare, it is important that you purchase Medicare Part C a/k/a Medicare Advantage which covers emergency and urgent care outside of the United States. Make sure that you either have a very high limit on the amount of coverage outside of the United States or no limit whatsoever. Note that this only covers emergency and urgent care and not for the long-term management of an illness such as cancer while you are in Country X. Medigap insurance will not cover care in Country X if you have been in Country X for 60 or more days.

Finally, if you are eligible for it, you can pay for medical coverage in the United States, such as a health plan offered under the requirements of the Affordable Care Act in the United States or Medicare Parts A, B, C and D. You can then couple your healthcare coverage in your country of origin with medical evacuation coverage that will allow you to get back to your country of origin no matter how ill or injured you may be.

IMPORTANT

Even if you have very good international private health insurance that is geared towards Country X, some private hospitals and healthcare professionals in Country X may not accept your insurance. If this happens to you, you may need to pay for your healthcare out-of-pocket, have any required paperwork filled out by the attending physician and then seek reimbursement directly from your insurer.

We do recommend that you consider purchasing IPMI if you are eligible for it, and it fits in your budget. The catch is that you may not be eligible for it, or any coverage you do receive might be limited in some way if it's determined that you have a pre-existing medical condition that excludes you from all or some coverage (see immediately below for a discussion on pre-existing conditions).

Preexisting Conditions and IPMI

International Medical/Health Insurance (IPMI) policies are typically medically underwritten. This means that a medical underwriter working for the insurance company will review your medical history and determine whether they will underwrite your coverage.

If they determine that a preexisting condition exists, the insurance company will usually take one of the following steps: (1) approve the application as is, (2) limit or exclude the preexisting condition, (3) add a premium to cover the additional risks associated with the preexisting conditions or (4) deny your application altogether.

Unfortunately, there is no way to find out what decision they will make in advance. This process might waste your time and cause you needless trouble, or it could be worth all the hassle. You simply must apply in order to find out what their decision will be.

"Are there reasons to maintain my public or private healthcare coverage in my country of origin even if I'm eligible for coverage in Country X?"

Yes, you may decide that you'll maintain your public or private health coverage in the United States even if you are eligible for health insurance in Country X for the following reasons:

• You might decide that you want to maintain your healthcare coverage in the United States so that you can receive cutting-edge medical treatments that are available in the United States but not available in Country X.

• You might decide that you want to maintain your healthcare coverage in your country of origin so that you can get treated near a loved one who can look after you during your treatment.

• You might decide that you want to maintain your healthcare coverage in your country of origin just in case you decide to leave Country X and return to the United States for any number of unforeseeable reasons.

Public and Private Networks

Both public and private healthcare systems have their own doctors, pharmacies, physicians, and healthcare regimes. These operate in independent networks. People are usually only allowed to use the services that are available within their network.

> **Key Things to Know**
>
> • The actual cost of your healthcare will vary depending on several factors including the nature of the hospital you visit, the seriousness of your condition and the hospital's location.
> • The best hospitals tend to be in the largest cities of the country. In the case of any major medical issue, the ideal approach would be to seek treatment in one of these locations.

For more resources and additional information to help you start an exciting new chapter in your life, please visit our website at www.AllPointsGuide.com.

12. BANKING & FINANCE

IN THIS CHAPTER, we focus on the banking and finance topics that you are most likely to face. We will help you to choose a financial institution that is right for you, and we will discuss the best ways to go about transferring money.

TRANSFERRING FUNDS & BANKING

Transferring Funds in General

Whenever you're transferring funds from your bank or other financial institutions in your country of origin to your bank or other financial institutions in Country X, it often makes sense to time the transfer carefully. On some occasions, it's better to transfer funds when the currency in your country of origin is stronger versus the peso than it usually is.

Banking: Country of Origin Accounts

Your current banking and/or investment institutions may be adequate to support your transnational lifestyle, but you may experience some headaches with them.

We encourage you to do some research into which financial institutions in your country of origin are best for someone living abroad. Even though we encourage you to open up an account in Country X, it might still be necessary from time to time to rely on your home bank for a credit/debit card.

You may find that some financial institutions offer better exchange rates or lower ATM fees or even reimburse you for any Country X ATM fees you may have incurred when withdrawing cash on your U.S. account.

If for some reason you do not want to use HSBC for your banking needs, the U.S. banks listed below have historically offered good value for international travelers.

If you live in the United States, Charles Schwab has offered, in the past, no foreign transaction fees and unlimited ATM fee rebates and, sometimes, no monthly service fees and no minimum balances.

Similarly, Capital One has offered, in the past, no maintenance or foreign transaction fees, and they may do so in the future.

TD Bank has offered, in the past, no foreign transaction fees and ATM-fee reimbursement with eligible accounts, and they may do so in the future.

Chime has offered, in the past, no monthly maintenance or foreign transaction fees with a simple checking account, and they may do so in the future.

NOTE: Transfers from any account in the world into Country X will result in a change of currency from one currency into the local Country X currency. This underscores the need to time transfers into the local currency at times when the local currency is weaker than usual against the U.S dollar. See the section on "TIMING YOUR TRANSFERS OF MONEY TO COUNTRY X" in Chapter 9 for more details about how to determine when transferring money into Country X benefits you.

Banking: Money Transfers

The cheapest way to send money from your U.S. bank account to your Country X bank account will likely be via an OFX Money Transfer.

You can set up rate alerts to send money when an exchange rate is more favorable for you. Delivery takes from one to four business days. OFX, however, has some limitations: The minimum you can send is $1,000, and transfers require bank accounts for sending and receiving money.

Possibly the most expedient and definitely the biggest network to use to send cash to yourself from your U.S. bank account is MoneyGram Money Transfer. You can pick up your local currency in-person AND you do not need to have a Country X bank account.

MoneyGram's convenience comes at a price. You'll pay at least $5 to send with cash, plus the exchange rate and markups. Sending from bank account to bank account is free other than what is lost due to the exchange rate.

The Foreign Account Tax Compliance Act (FATCA) (United States)

FATCA was passed as part of the HIRE Act in 2010 (Public Law No. 111-147). It may require that certain foreign financial institutions report information on their accounts that have ties to the United States. This might mean that, if you are a U.S. citizen, your Country X bank might be required to supply information about you to the U.S. government. They do this to make sure that you are not hiding your income tax obligations or any other kind of tax obligations from the IRS. FATCA may also require that certain non-financial foreign entities, such as a corporation that is not a bank or involved in finance in any way, must report information regarding you or even be subject to withholding on applicable payments that are owed to you by those entities.

The Possibility of a Meltdown of the U.S. Dollar

One thing to consider is the possible devaluation of the U.S. dollar. To the extent that your income or assets are tied to that currency, it could make living in Country X less affordable. We are simply raising this as a possibility to consider, and you might decide to diversify your income and assets across more than one country as a hedge against that happening.

Mutual Funds and U.S. Citizens Living Overseas

Charles Schwab and Company, Fidelity Investment and T. Rowe Price have announced that they will no longer allow Americans living overseas, even in the case of their own employees, to buy U.S.-based mutual funds.

There are limited exceptions for 401k plans, but for all other accounts including IRAs and Brokerage accounts, whether self-managed, with the company as the advisor or with an independent investment advisor, mutual fund purchases (including dividend re-investments) have come to a halt.

Charles Schwab and Company, Fidelity Investment and T. Rowe Price are not forcing clients to sell the mutual funds they already own (because that would force a capital gain or loss) and are not, for the most part, forcing accounts to be closed, but they are limiting new purchases.

The good news is that there is no prohibition against Americans living overseas purchasing exchange traded funds (ETFs), and there is a very good chance that you will easily find ETF versions of your favorite mutual funds, effectively eliminating the need to purchase mutual funds.

An exchange traded fund is like a mutual fund in most respects. Like mutual funds, ETFs allow you to purchase a bundle of stocks or a bundle of bonds rather than purchasing stocks or bonds singly. There may, however, be some taxation issues and other differences between mutual funds and ETFs so be sure to check with your competent financial, legal and tax advisors before purchasing shares in ETFs.

Credit History

Unless you plan to pay for everything you want to purchase in Country X in cash (not on credit or via financing), you may need to develop a credit history in Country X. Your credit history in your country of origin may not transfer to Country X. You might consider getting a Country X credit card to start cultivating a Country X credit history and score.

FINANCING A HOME IN COUNTRY X

Many foreigners that purchase a home in Country X will pay cash outright rather than using financing. They typically use the proceeds of the sale of their home in the U.S. as the source for the purchase money. It is possible, however, to obtain funding through a variety of sources, based on your foreign income. These kinds of loans are called cross-border mortgages.

In some cases, cross-border mortgages are often offered directly through local banks that have a close affiliation with a U.S.

It might be advantageous to use a broker who can help guide you through the process and increase your chances of getting the best deal possible. Note that some brokers may choose to only work with U.S. citizens. To find one, do a google search with the terms: cross-border mortgage broker [Country X]. It will be easier to find a U.S. broker dealing with countries that are in closer geographic proximity to the U.S. rather than farther away.

No matter what type of financing you use, it is important to note that foreign mortgage interest payments may qualify for a deduction on your U.S. tax returns. Be sure to check with your U.S. tax and legal professionals.

GETTING IDENTIFICATION NUMBERS

Just as foreigners in the United States obtain social security numbers, make sure that you obtain all of the local identification numbers that you might need to function in Country X.

☆ ☆ ☆ ☆ ☆

For more resources and additional information to help you start an exciting new chapter in your life, please visit our website at www.AllPointsGuide.com.

13. REAL ESTATE

FOR SOME, this might be the most helpful chapter in this book because it can help you make a smarter decision by providing a detailed analysis about whether to buy or rent a home in Country X. The decision to buy or rent is often a very personal decision and sometimes an emotional one. We do not intend to make this decision for you but rather seek to provide you with all of the information we can so that you can make the most informed decision possible.

We cover a wide variety of topics, but let's deal with one question that a lot of people have about Country X right away.

YOUR HOME IN YOUR COUNTRY OF ORIGIN

You basically have 3 options with regard to the real estate you own in your country of origin: sell it, rent it out or keep it vacant. There may be a variety of legal, tax and financial issues associated with each option. We recommend that you talk to your advisors before doing anything.

Capital Gains Tax Issues (U.S.)

NOTE: If you are a resident of the United States, you'll want to weigh the potential benefit of selling your home before moving to Country X, and then using your $250,000 home sale exclusion (or $500,000 total exclusion for a couple) to avoid or minimize your U.S. capital gains taxes.

For U.S. residents, if you move out of your home, your eligibility for the U.S. home sale exclusion begins to diminish. This happens because you are required to have used the home as your primary residence for at least 730 days (24 months) total at some point in the five years immediately preceding the closing date of your home's sale. If you are half of a married couple, both spouses must have individually used the property for 24 out of the last 60 months in order to qualify for the full principal residence exclusion.

If you as a couple move to Country X and you have been living in your home for the past 2 years, you will need to sell the property within the next three years to get the exclusion. If you miss this 2-years-in-5 window, then you would need to find a way to move back into your home and live in the property for two additional years in order to regain your ability to benefit from this tax incentive. Moving back to your country of origin may, however, defeat your goal of living in Country X.

Alternatively, if you have gains that substantially exceed the amount you can exclude, you might consider renting out your American home and then getting a step-up in the basis upon your death. This step-up in basis would allow your heirs to sell your home free of capital gains tax, with the possible exception of any gains that occurred after the date-of-death valuation of the property.

One potential downside of continuing to own your home in your home country is that it can be viewed by the state in which it is located to be proof that you are still domiciled in that state. If you are trying to convince a state that you no longer live in it, then selling your home might help to convince them that you have moved.

Before you rent out your home to anyone, make sure that your home has adequate insurance coverage.

GATED COMMUNITIES VS. UNGATED COMMUNITIES

Pros of Gated Communities:

(1) A gated community can make you feel secure and may, if the security measures are properly done, actually increase your level of security.

(2) There may be less traffic on the streets within the community than there would otherwise be.

(3) A gated community may increase the property values of the homes within its gates.

Cons of Gated Communities:

(1) On average, gated communities may not actually confer any extra security; although there may be some gated communities with much tighter security than others that actually do confer greater security.

(2) The cost of extra security, even if spread among many homeowners, can significantly increase your cost of living.

(3) It might make it difficult for deliveries or even emergency services to get through to you.

(4) Your guests may get annoyed with the extra procedures and the invasiveness of going through a security checkpoint.

(5) Whenever there is a queue of vehicles trying to get into the gated community, it can add several minutes to your travel time or the travel time of your visitors, delivery people and service providers.

(6) In general, it might leave less room for spontaneity and autonomy.

RENTING VS. BUYING YOUR HOME IN COUNTRY X

Evaluating whether it's in your best interest to purchase real estate in Country X rather than simply rent a place in Country X is a major life decision. There are many factors in favor of either approach as well as many factors against either approach.

Possible Advantages of Renting:

• You avoid a hefty transfer tax or "acquisition tax," closing costs, financing costs, fees of the *notario*, etc. associated with buying real estate.

• If the local currency of Country X is devalued you are not stuck holding real estate that is tied to the local currency and to the local economy.

• If the source of your water supply becomes scarce or unavailable or simply more expensive than you can easily afford, you can simply move to an area where water is more plentiful.

• If climate change makes the place where you are living less enjoyable due to flooding, you would have the option of simply moving to an area that is less adversely affected by climate change.

• Every dollar that is money tied up in Country X real estate is a dollar that could give you a better return on your investment (ROI) if invested elsewhere. Note: This assumes that the Country X real estate you would have purchased isn't appreciating very rapidly.

• If there are any latent or hidden defects in the title of the property, it shouldn't affect you.

• If there are any defects in the building itself, such as termite or other kinds of infestations, wet rot, dry rot, plumbing problems, electrical problems, proximity to loud noises, etc., then you can simply move to a new place.

• You might find that you do not like your neighbors. For instance, some people move into a place where they are surrounded by expats and then realize that they would rather live in a neighborhood that is more diverse. Alternatively, you might find that your neighbors view you as the rich foreigner and are constantly asking you for money and so you decide that you want to live somewhere that is more solidly middle-class. If you are renting, then you can simply move if it turns out that you do not like your neighbors.

• You can leave your home vacant for long stretches of time without worrying about the possibility that squatters might move into it or thieves might strip it of its copper wiring, etc. This is an especially important consideration if you live several months a year outside of Country X.

• By renting rather than buying, you might be avoiding the possibility of a home taking years to sell.

• If your rental is damaged by a natural disaster, it is the owner who will bear the costs rather than you. In fact, you could just leave and find a home that is not damaged to rent (even if it means losing a deposit).

• You are U.S. taxpayer and plan to file Form 2555 in an attempt to exclude your foreign income under the FEIE (see Chapter 14). Owning your home in a country that could tax your foreign income could cause such a country to tax your foreign income and make it impossible for you to benefit from any possible tax benefits of the FEIE, the Foreign Housing Exclusion or the Foreign Housing Deduction.

• You are a U.S. taxpayer and seek to pay taxes in the United States (rather than in a country that can tax your foreign income) in order to increase your potential Social Security benefits. Owning your home in a country that might tax your foreign income could cause such a country to tax your income and decrease the amount that you can pay towards U.S. taxes (which might ultimately increase your Social Security benefits).

Possible Disadvantages of Renting:

• If property values increase dramatically, then you'll be missing out on the appreciating value of your home. As a result, you may be subject to higher rents that you're less able to afford due to increased housing costs. In short, you could be priced out of the home you had been renting.

• If you plan to live in the same home for decades, then renting, compared to buying, may provide you with an inferior economic outcome in the long run.

• You might have a landlord who is difficult to deal with.

• You might have a landlord who asks for excessive increases in rent.

• You might have a landlord who neglects the property in which you are living.

• You might have a landlord who decides to terminate the lease before you wish to move out. If you are elderly or disabled, any disruption in your living situation could be extremely difficult and so you may decide to purchase a home for this reason alone.

• A devaluation of the U.S. dollar that does not result in a devaluation of the local currency could make your decision to not purchase a home in Country X look like a missed opportunity.

• A big increase in human lifespan due to advances in medicine may make renting for the rest of your life more expensive than purchasing a home.

Possible Advantages of Buying:

• A devaluation of the U.S. dollar that does not result in a devaluation of the local Country X currency could make your purchase of real estate in Country X look like an excellent investment.

• If property values increase dramatically during your ownership of the property, then you may be able to profit from your ownership.

• You avoid having a landlord (who may have wanted to increase the rent excessively, terminate the lease, refuse to make repairs and upgrades or ask for a guarantor or guaranty, see discussion on guarantors and guaranties below).

• You may be able to renovate and improve the property so that it better suits your needs and then possibly recoup some or all of the costs of any repairs and/or upgrades you make during your stay upon the sale of the property.

• Even if housing prices go up in your neighborhood or the general area in which your property is located, your housing costs might remain relatively constant, and that could save you money over the long run.

• You might be able to rent out your home (all or part of it) on a short-term or long-term basis.

• A big increase in the human lifespan due to advances in medicine may make purchasing a home less expensive than renting for the rest of your life.

Possible Disadvantages of Buying:

• You will likely pay a hefty transfer tax or "acquisition tax," closing costs, financing costs, fees of attorneys and/or title companies, etc.

• A devaluation of the local currency could reduce the value of your home relative to the amount of dollars you put into it.

• Hotter and/or more humid weather, more frequent or intense hurricanes and other changes due to climate change could make your home less livable and/or more dangerous. This could dramatically reduce the value of your home and make it more difficult to find a buyer for your home should you decide to relocate.

• Your water supply could become scarce or unavailable or painfully expensive due to drought or some other reason. This could dramatically reduce the value of your home, especially if the price of water where you live becomes astronomically expensive and make it more difficult to find a buyer for your home should you decide to relocate.

• An upswing in criminal activity or political unrest in the vicinity of your home could make your home less livable and/or more dangerous, decreasing the value of your home yet making you want to relocate.

• If there are any latent or hidden defects in the building itself, such as termite or other kinds of infestations, wet rot, dry rot, plumbing problems, electrical problems, the home would then require rehabilitation involving your own time, money and aggravation to improve those conditions.

• There may be a "cloud" on your title to the home and any title insurance policy you might have purchased might have carved out an exception to that particular defect of title.

• You might find that you do not like your neighbors.

• Keeping a large portion of your assets in local currency (or physically tied up in local real estate) runs the risk of a devaluation of the local currency. Keeping your assets in U.S. dollars or U.S. equities may better maintain or increase the value of those assets. It's important to note that there's no guarantee that the local currency will become devalued even if there's a history of that happening.

• Another reason why buying might be a bad idea is that there may need to be an estate administration on your property when you die which creates additional expenses, delays and hassles.

• If you leave your home vacant for long stretches of time there is the possibility that squatters might move into it or thieves might strip it of your belongings, copper wiring, etc. This is an important consideration if you live several months a year outside of Country X.

• There is a possibility that a home that you might have purchased will take years to sell before you find a buyer to purchase the property at a good price.

• Natural disasters: If your home is damaged by a natural disaster, you have to deal with repairs and if the expenses are not covered by insurance, then the cost of repairs will have to be covered by you.

• If you are U.S. taxpayer and plan to file Form 2555 in an attempt to exclude your foreign income under the FEIE (see Chapter 14), owning your home in a country that might tax your foreign income could cause such a country to tax your foreign income. If that happens, it would be impossible to benefit from the tax benefits of the FEIE, the Foreign Housing Exclusion and/or the Foreign Housing Deduction.

• If you are a U.S. taxpayer and seek to pay taxes to the U.S. in order to maximize your potential Social Security benefits, then owning a home in a country that might tax foreign income could increase the possibility that such a country will choose to tax your income and potentially reduce the amount of U.S. taxes that you are paying.

Conclusion on Renting vs. Buying

Renting is likely to be preferable over buying for the majority of people from other countries seeking to live in Country X after they do a careful analysis of the factors listed above. On the other hand, if you seek to live in a place in Country X that has historically enjoyed rapid gains in property values or if you plan to keep your Country X home for multiple decades or multiple generations, then buying might be preferable.

Another reason that buying might be advantageous is if you plan to purchase a property in order to be eligible for a residency visa. Having said that, if you have the means to purchase a qualifying property in Country X, then you probably have the income or assets necessary to obtain a residency visa without purchasing a home in Country X.

IMPORTANT NOTE

If you decide that you do want to buy a home in Country X, we recommend that you first rent a home close to your desired location for a couple of months to "test the waters" and make sure it is the right location and lifestyle for you.

How to Rent a Home Through Airbnb

AirBnb.com is a wonderful resource for renters for several reasons, even if it seems like the prices are much higher:

1. It provides a turn-key living space that **includes furniture** and **utilities** that might save you a great deal of time, trouble and money.

2. You can evaluate a property based on the reviews it has received. NOTE: Make sure the positive reviews evaluate the property itself and not just the owner. Otherwise, it's possible that they did not like the property but developed a personal connection with the owner and did not want to hurt that person in the evaluation process.

3. You can rent for a number of days or save money by renting for a number of months. If you rent the same listing for 29 days or more, you might unlock a lower monthly rate if one has been set.

4. You are paying by credit card and so are racking up points, miles or other rewards from your credit card company.

5. If you plan to rent for several months to 1 year or more, you can send the owner or manager of the property a message and find out if they are willing to negotiate a lower monthly rent based on your commitment to a longer-term rental.

6. The hosts may provide insurance coverage and so there is a chance that you or your estate would be able to successfully sue the host for any damages.

INSURANCE ON REAL ESTATE IN COUNTRY X

Home Insurance

If you decide to purchase a home in Country X, you will want to purchase homeowner's insurance for it. Do not, however, assume that your Country X homeowner's policy is identical to the homeowner's policy you once purchased in your country of origin. The policy wording is unique, and the types of coverage offered by insurance companies is possibly different in Country X. Depending upon where you live, you may want to get coverage for such risks as earthquakes, hurricanes and flooding.

Title Insurance

Title insurance covers you in the event that the title deed of the property you purchase turns out to be invalid causing your right to the property to be brought into question and pays out compensation in the event that you lose title to the home you purchased.

Rental Insurance

If you decide to rent a home rather than buy one, you may want to consider renter's insurance to insure your own personal property.

☆ ☆ ☆ ☆ ☆

For more resources and additional information to help you start an exciting new chapter in your life, please visit our website at www.AllPointsGuide.com.

14. TAX ISSUES

IF THIS CHAPTER can save you tens of thousands of dollars per year on taxes, then it is certainly one of the most important chapters in the book. Please read this chapter very carefully, perhaps more than once, to see if there are any ways that you can substantially reduce your tax burden. Obviously, there are no guarantees that this chapter can aid you in saving tens of thousands of dollars a year on taxes, but it is worth a careful investigation to see if it might. Talking to tax professionals in Country X and in any other country where you are currently deemed to be a taxpayer or tax resident is an excellent idea. Note that some of the possible tax savings discussed in this chapter *only apply* to eligible *U.S.* taxpayers.

THE POSSIBLE NEED TO FILE TAXES IN THE U.S.

If you have maintained your citizenship in the U.S., you MAY need to file taxes in the U.S. EVEN IF NO TAXES ARE DUE IN THE U.S. Depending on what your tax professionals in Country X advise, you may also need to file taxes in Country X. If you are from the United States, you will generally be considered a U.S. taxpayer for life no matter where you live, and you will be expected to file a tax return even if no taxes are due to the U.S.

DOUBLE TAXATION

Double taxation occurs when you are required to pay taxes on the same income twice: once in the U.S. and once in the country in which you are residing.

It is important that you check to make sure that the country you want to live in has a double taxation treaty with the U.S. Also, find out what the exact terms are because not all double taxation treaties provide the same advantages to taxpayers.

"What are tax treaties?"

The United States has tax treaties with a number of foreign countries. Under these treaties, residents (who do not necessarily have to be citizens) of foreign countries are taxed at a reduced rate, or are exempt from United States taxes, on certain items of income they receive from sources within the United States. These reduced rates and exemptions vary from country to country and on the specific types of income that they cover.

At the same time, residents or citizens of the United States are taxed at a reduced rate, or are exempt from foreign taxes, on certain items of income they receive from sources within foreign countries under these same treaties. Most income tax treaties include what is known as a "saving clause," which prevents a citizen or resident of the United States from using the provisions of a tax treaty in order to avoid taxation of US-source income.

The U.S. Has Tax Treaties with These Countries

Armenia	Iceland	Philippines
Australia	India	Poland
Austria	Indonesia	Portugal
Azerbaijan	Ireland	Romania
Bangladesh	Israel	Russia
Barbados	Italy	Slovak Republic
Belarus	Jamaica	Slovenia
Belgium	Japan	South Africa
Bulgaria	Kazakhstan	Spain
Canada	Korea	Sri Lanka
China	Kyrgyzstan	Sweden
Cyprus	Latvia	Switzerland
Czech Republic	Lithuania	Tajikistan
Denmark	Luxembourg	Thailand
Egypt	Malta	Trinidad
Estonia	Mexico	Tunisia
Finland	Moldova	Turkey
France	Morocco	Turkmenistan
Georgia	Netherlands	Ukraine
Germany	New Zealand	United Kingdom
Greece	Norway	Uzbekistan
Hungary	Pakistan	Venezuela

NOTE: You will want to research the terms and substance of each tax treaty. Not all tax treaties are the same or offer the same level of protection for U.S. taxpayers.

TOTALIZATION AGREEMENTS

"Totalization Agreements," also referred to as "bilateral agreements," eliminate dual social security coverage, which is the situation that occurs when a person from one country works in another country and is required to pay social security taxes to both countries on the same earnings.

The U.S. Has Totalization Treaties with These Countries

Austria	Germany	Poland
Australia	Greece	Portugal
Belgium	Hungary	Slovak Republic
Brazil	Iceland	Slovenia
Canada	Ireland	South Korea
Chile	Italy	Spain
Czech Republic	Japan	Switzerland
Denmark	Luxembourg	United Kingdom
Finland	Netherlands	Uruguay
France	Norway	Sweden

FOREIGN TAX CREDIT (FTC) FOR U.S. EXPATS

The Foreign Tax Credit (FTC) is one method U.S. expats can use to offset foreign taxes paid abroad on a dollar-for-dollar basis, and its availability follows from the double taxation treaties between the United States and other countries.

It requires you to file Form 1116 with your tax return. Before you invoke the FTC, however, make sure that it is the best option for you, especially if you are also eligible to invoke the Foreign Earned Income Exclusion or the FEIE (which is discussed below).

As an example of how the FTC works, if you owe the U.S. government, say, $2,500 in taxes and you have a $500 tax credit, you'll end up only paying $2,000 to the IRS. The maximum credit amount you're allowed to claim depends on your worldwide income and how much in taxes you've already paid.

"Am I eligible for the FTC?"

In general, you're eligible for the credit if you're a U.S. citizen or resident who earns foreign income abroad and already paid income taxes to your new country of residence.

Often expats will owe no U.S. tax if working in a country with a higher tax rate than the U.S., like China, but the rules are complex depending on the country where you live and the foreign tax credit limitations. That's why it's critical that you work with your U.S. expat tax advisor to find out which foreign taxes you can use to maximize your FTC.

Foreign Tax Credit Limitations & Rules for U.S. Citizens Abroad

There are a few foreign tax credit limitations for U.S. expats. You can't just claim it on any income earned abroad. In order to claim the credit:

• The tax must be imposed on you. If paying taxes to Country X is in any way voluntary, then you won't qualify for the FTC.

• You must have already paid or accrued the foreign tax. If you haven't paid it, accrued it or are not responsible for paying it, then you cannot assert the FTC.

• The tax must be the legal and actual foreign tax liability. It cannot be a mere estimate.

• The tax must be an income tax (or a tax in lieu of an income tax). Payment of a transfer tax, for example, will not qualify.

The IRS has identified the following types of foreign taxes as not being eligible for the FTC:

• Taxes on excluded income (for example, if you've already used the foreign earned income exclusion)

• Taxes refundable to you

• Taxes paid to a foreign country deemed to support international terrorism

• Taxes for which you can only take an itemized deduction

• Taxes on foreign mineral income

• Taxes from international boycott operations

• A portion of taxes on combined foreign oil and gas income

• Taxes related to a foreign tax-splitting event

• Social security taxes paid or accrued to a foreign country with which the United States has a social security agreement.

There is an exception to the rule that only income tax counts towards an FTC. This exception was created to accommodate taxpayers that live in countries that do not have an income tax, such as the United Arab Emirates, but have other forms of taxes. If you paid foreign taxes in lieu of income taxes, you still may be able to offset them with the FTC. Taxes that qualify must be a foreign levy imposed in place of an income tax. Each scenario in each country is different.

Foreign Tax Credit Carryover

One convenient thing about claiming the FTC is the foreign tax credit carryover. Essentially, the carryover means that if you don't use the full tax credit amount that is rightfully yours for a given tax year, then your unused amount can carry over to the next tax year or carry back to the previous year. If you were short on credits in the previous year, your leftover amount must be carried back.

For example, if you have a $600 carryover amount and in the previous year you were short $700 in credits on foreign income, you must carryback that $600 to that previous year instead of carrying it forward. If you are allowed to carry it over, your tax credit carryover can be carried over for up to 10 years.

Calculating Your Tax Credit and Carryover Amount

To get your maximum credit amount you'll divide your foreign-sourced taxable income amount by your total taxable income, then multiply that result by your U.S. tax liability.

FOREIGN EARNED INCOME EXCLUSION FOR U.S. EXPATS

The Foreign Earned Income Exclusion (FEIE) is one of the greatest tax benefits available to U.S. citizens living abroad. If you're eligible, it will enable you to exclude all or a portion of your foreign earned income from your U.S. taxes. And as long as Country X does not view you as a taxable resident of Country X, you may not owe any taxes on your excluded income to either country (other than what the United States requires you to pay as a bare minimum for FICA purposes on your self-employment income).

Unlike the Foreign Tax Credit described above, the FEIE works even if Country X decides to not tax you.

Key Things to Know about the FEIE

• If you are eligible and you properly file your tax return with the IRS, the FEIE might save you **tens of thousands of dollars** on your U.S. taxes.

• It does not allow you to exclude **all** types of income.

• You need to meet specific qualifications and *then* file the proper paperwork (Form 2555)

• If you are eligible for FEIE, it does not necessarily mean that Country X will not tax you on any income eligible for Country X taxation. That is a separate question.

• The FEIE isn't your only tax relief option. Talk to your U.S. tax professional about every aspect of your financial situation including your housing costs (see below for a discussion on the Foreign Housing Exclusion).

The types of income that MIGHT NOT COUNT TOWARDS THE FEIE:

• Social Security benefits, annuities, pension benefits and retirement account distributions
• interest
• dividends

The kinds of income that MIGHT COUNT TOWARDS THE FEIE INCLUDE:

- Salary
- Wages
- Bonuses
- Commissions
- SELF-EMPLOYMENT INCOME

Even income paid to you by U.S. employers, clients and customers may be eligible for the FEIE. The key is that you were living in Country X or in multiple countries at the time of earning those salaries, wages, bonuses, commissions and self-employment dollars, and did the lion's share of the work from outside the United States.

There are two tests used to determine if you satisfy the obligation of living outside of the U.S., and you only need to pass one of them: Bona Fide Residency Test or the Physical Presence Test.

How to Pass the Bona Fide Residency Test

In order to pass the Bona Fide Residence Test, you need to adequately demonstrate that you have more connections to a foreign country than the U.S. You also must be a resident of that country for an uninterrupted period that includes an entire tax year. When and if you go back to the U.S., you must have the intention of returning to your current foreign country of residence. In addition, you must:

- Be a U.S. citizen or be a resident alien of a foreign country with which the U.S. has an income tax treaty.
- Generate active income. Unearned (or money earned in prior tax years) or inactive income like pension payouts, Social Security benefits,

retirement account distributions, interest and dividends cannot be included.

- Be overseas for work for a period longer than a year.
- Have a permanent place of work in a foreign country.

It is possible to be a Bona Fide Resident for part of the year if you spent at least a full tax year outside the U.S. in a prior year. If you do so, you would only be able to claim the FEIE for the part of the year that you were living in Country X.

How to Pass the Physical Presence Test

In order to qualify under the Physical Presence Test, you must have been living outside the U.S. for 330 full days out of the year. Note that this does not require you to spend all 330 days outside of the U.S. You can spend time in as many countries as you like, other than the U.S.

Be careful when you track your time because a "full day" counts as 24 hours starting at midnight, and you need to be in-country for every minute of those 24 hours.

For example, if you lived in Tijuana and jaunted across the border to San Diego for Friday night and came back Saturday evening, you wouldn't be able to count either Friday or Saturday towards your 330 full days.

Remember that you only need to pass one test. For most people, the Physical Presence Test will be the easier of the two as, in the event you are audited, you may only need to show the stamps in your passport to prove you met the requirements of the test.

"How much foreign income can I exclude?"

If you qualify for the FEIE on your U.S. taxes, you may be able to exclude up to $112,000 per person for your tax year 2022 filing. The number is tied to inflation. For tax year 2023, the number jumps up to $120,000 per person.

NOTE: In the event that you're married and both you and your spouse meet either the bona fide residency test or the physical presence test, you may each be eligible for the FEIE, essentially doubling the exclusion.

"Are there any drawbacks to using the FEIE?"

Yes, the following are some possible drawbacks to using the FEIE:

• You may not be eligible to contribute to an individual retirement arrangement (IRA) if you apply for the FEIE (and any foreign housing exclusion) unless your total income exceeds the total excluded amount.

• The FEIE does not exclude or reduce taxes on passive or investment income. If all of your income is coming from pension payouts, Social Security benefits, retirement account distributions, interest and dividends, then filing for the FEIE is probably NOT the right approach.

• You must live outside the U.S. for most or all of the year.

• Employees of the U.S. government can't claim the FEIE. This restriction applies to military personnel and embassy personnel living abroad. An employee of a private company under contract with the U.S. government, however, might still be eligible.

Common Problems U.S. Expats Have with the Foreign Income Exclusion and Form 2555

If you think you're eligible for the FEIE but you do not receive the FEIE or do not get the BEST RESULT on your net taxes, here are some common reasons why that may have happened:

• You didn't file Form 2555. Many expats wrongly think that if they qualify for the FEIE it will be automatically added to their tax filing. In order to claim the FEIE and benefit from it you must file Form 2555.

• You're a U.S. government employee and, therefore, aren't eligible for the FEIE. This limitation applies to active-duty military personnel stationed overseas and embassy personnel working outside the United States, among others.

• You failed to calculate the FEIE accurately. If you calculate your FEIE incorrectly you may not get the correct amount excluded.

• You claimed the FEIE when you should have claimed the FTC. For example, if you're retired abroad and you only have investment and passive income, you may have been better off claiming the FTC, even if you are making a little bit of money from self-employment during your retirement.

•You didn't track your time properly. You must be rigorous about tracking your time if you want to pass the Bona Fide Residency or Physical Presence tests. Even getting it wrong by a few hours can upend your eligibility for the FEIE.

• You had no active income for that year. If you're living abroad off investment or passive income, you don't qualify for the FEIE.

• You didn't pay your U.S. self-employment taxes such as FICA that go towards funding Social Security retirement, disability, survivor, spousal and children's benefits, as well as a big chunk of Medicare's budget. The IRS still requires you to pay any self-employment taxes that may be due such as FICA when you're claiming the FEIE. Typically, the self-employment tax rate is 15.3%, which includes: 12.4% for social security (old-age, survivors, and disability insurance) and 2.9% for Medicare (hospital insurance).

• You didn't pay your STATE income taxes. The FEIE only applies to your FEDERAL income tax obligations and not to your STATE income tax obligations (see below for a discussion of state income taxes).

"Should I use the Foreign Tax Credit or the Foreign Earned Income Exclusion?"

The downside to these two wonderful options (the Foreign Tax Credit and the Foreign Earned Income Exclusion) is that you cannot do both. You must choose between the FTC and the FEIE. It's important to note that the choice only comes into play if Country X is going to tax you on your income. If Country X is not going to tax you, then you should simply opt for the FEIE because that will reduce your taxes the most and because the FTC is simply not an option. For the reasons discussed above, the FTC is only an option if Country X IS going to tax you.

On the other hand, if Country X IS going to tax you on the amount of money that is excluded under the FEIE, then it's important to choose between the FTC and the FEIE cleverly and after serious deliberations. The main reason for this is that if you claim the FEIE and then change back to the FTC, you can't claim the FEIE again for five years. The only way to claim the FEIE again involves a pricey process with the IRS. Working with an expat tax advisor in the U.S. to help you shape your decision between the FTC and the FEIE, provided that you have to make the choice, would be a very good idea.

If you end up claiming the FTC, it is best to do so if any of the following circumstances apply:

• You're paying tax in Country X at a higher rate than your U.S. tax rate.

• You seek to make new contributions to an individual retirement arrangement (IRA).

• You qualify for certain family-related credits based on non-excluded income.

• You seek to exclude or reduce taxes on passive or investment income.

FOREIGN HOUSING EXCLUSION OR DEDUCTION FOR U.S. CITIZENS ELIGIBLE FOR FEIE

If you're an expat and you incur foreign housing expenses, you might be able to exclude or deduct them. It depends on whether you are an EMPLOYEE or are SELF-EMPLOYED.

The Foreign Housing Exclusion is available for expats working as EMPLOYEES with housing expenses like rent and utilities.

The Foreign Housing Deduction, on the other hand, is available for SELF-EMPLOYED EXPATS paying foreign housing expenses. The amount of your housing exclusion or deduction is based on the difference between the following:

• Your actual foreign housing expenses

• A base amount for your foreign country of residence

You can use the Foreign Housing Exclusion if your housing costs total more than 16% of that year's FEIE.

To calculate the maximum amount you can exclude, you'd multiply that year's maximum income exclusion by 0.3 to get 30% of the full exclusion amount. So, for 2023, you'd take $120,000 x 0.3 = $36,000. Something to know is that most large metro areas have higher limits, so it's important to have a U.S. expat tax advisor who knows the nitty gritty details of taxes in your specific area.

NOTE: The IRS does not allow you to "double dip" by excluding the same income twice between both an FEIE and a Foreign Housing Exclusion. Your income can only be excluded once. For this reason, it is best to get professional help when figuring out how to fill out Form 2555 and how to allocate any tax benefits for which you might be eligible.

THE OTHER DAYS OF THE YEAR

Let's say you can only spend 179 days of the year in Country X without be viewed as a tax resident. Where do you spend the remaining days of any given 12-month rolling period before returning to Mexico?

For some people, returning home to the United States might be how they want to spend those remaining days. Unfortunately, if you are a U.S. taxpayer seeking eligibility for the FEIE, the Foreign Housing Exclusion or the Foreign Housing Deduction, then returning to the U.S. might make you ineligible for any of those exclusions and/or deductions. This is because you need to satisfy the requirements of either the Bona Fide Residency Test or the Physical Presence Test (see above for more information the FEIE, the Bona Fide Residency Test and the Physical Presence Test) in order to maintain your eligibility for the FEIE and other exclusions and/or deductions.

You would, therefore, spend the other days of that rolling 12-month period in another country outside of the United States making sure that your foreign income will not be subject to tax in that other country.

SHORT-TERM RENTING

If you are a U.S. taxpayer, and you want to pay into the Social Security system to maximize your benefits, or if you plan to take advantage of the Foreign Earned Income Exclusion and possibly an exclusion or deduction of your housing expenses, then you may want to take the following measures to minimize your risk of being treated as a tax resident of Mexico: Rent a home in Country X for not more than, say, 179 days per 12-month rolling period and seek foreign (outside of Country X) sources of income. Short-term rentals from AirBnB would be ideal for this.

Possible Disadvantages

It is important to note that not purchasing a home in Country X may come with some drawbacks (see Chapter 13: Renting vs. Buying Your Home in Mexico for a further discussion of the potential advantages and disadvantages that might come with either buying or renting a home in Mexico) that might outweigh any potential tax benefits.

No Guarantees

There are no guarantees that taking any step mentioned in this book will prevent you from being treated by Country X as a tax resident. We are giving you information so that you can minimize your chances of being viewed as a tax resident by countries that tax the foreign income of their tax residents. Also, be sure to confirm all this information with your own tax advisors who are aware of your own unique circumstances.

PAYING TAX IN COUNTRY X VS. THE UNITED STATES

People are often given the advice that they should shift their income from the United States to another country so that they can pay less tax. Let's attempt to answer the following question:

"Should I shift my income from the United States to Country X?"

If you're a United States citizen working as a "digital nomad" in Country X, you might have received advice like this: "Shift your income from the United States to Country X in order to avoid paying Federal Insurance Contribution Act (FICA) payroll taxes that fund the Social Security and Medicare systems."

The idea that some propose is to create a Country X corporation, have your employer(s) and/or customer(s) pay money to the Country X corporation and then have the Country X corporation pay you so that you can sidestep paying the FICA taxes on all earnings.

We do not recommend that you do this. If you decide that you want to do it anyway, it's IMPERATIVE that you talk to legal, financial and tax experts in both the United States and Country X before you do anything along these lines so that you understand all of the consequences that might result from this course of action.

Here are some facts to consider that may make you decide against shifting income in this manner to a Country X corporation:

1. Paying money into the Social Security system allows you to build up credits that you may someday need to allow you to "cash out" of in the form of benefits, including monthly Social Security benefits in your retirement but also Social Security Disability Insurance if you are ever disabled. Even after you have accumulated the minimum number of credits you need to receive Social Security benefits (40 credits), the more you pay into these programs, the more you can get out of them (up to the maximum limit).

2. Paying money into the Social Security system in order to reach a minimum of 40 credits is necessary OR you risk not getting any Social Security benefits at all. To find out if you have reached this minimal requirement, you can log into your account with the Social Security Administration and check your Social Security statement here (and have your legal/tax/benefits team look it over for you):

https://www.ssa.gov/myaccount/statement.html

3. Any tax savings you might gain by shifting income to Country X to avoid paying into federal programs might be offset by a possible increased marginal tax rate on the Country X side of the equation. A comparatively greater tax rate in Country X may be especially true if you are able to establish legal residency, for income tax purposes, in a state in the United States that has no state income tax. This is because you would be further knocking down your total taxes if you pay taxes on the U.S. side of the border.

To see the difference between your marginal tax in the United States and in Country X, you can use a tax calculator like this one:

https://www.irscalculators.com/international-tax-calculator

This calculator does not do a side-by-side calculation so you will need to first calculate your United States marginal tax rate first, write it down and then calculate your Country X marginal tax rate.

4. Setting up and maintaining a Country X corporation and doing a Country X tax return each year will come with its own set of hassles, time sinks, costs and fees that might offset any savings and fees.

5. There's no guarantee that the IRS will be convinced that the income that your Country X corporation is receiving isn't income that is taxable by the United States. The last thing you want is to have the IRS prosecute you for dodging a U.S. tax liability.

6. If you later decide that you want to leave Country X for another country, you are saddled with a whole Country X-oriented infrastructure from which you will need to dismantle. And you will need to convince Country X that you are no longer a Country X taxpayer. You do not want to have any trailing Country X tax liabilities.

7. Compare this approach with filing for the FEIE. The fact that you are not paying tax on your foreign income in Country X means that you may be eligible to benefit from the FEIE, the Foreign Housing Deduction and/or the Foreign Housing Exclusion.

STATE INCOME TAX

In addition to determining if you need to keep paying income tax to the Treasury Department (IRS), you need to determine which, if any, state income tax you will need to pay.

If you decide, like many people, that it doesn't make sense to pay state income tax to a state that you don't even live in, then you might consider taking steps to decouple yourself from your current state and "migrate" to a state with *no* state income tax. The first step to do so is to set up a virtual address.

"What Is a Virtual Address?"

A virtual address is an actual street address rather than just a PO box that is owned and maintained by a third party. Let us say that you choose to establish residency in South Dakota. You would pay a fee to a company that would provide you with a street address.

The companies that provide you with a virtual address receive mail on your behalf and then provide three possible services depending on the type of mail you receive. The first service they provide is to scan letters they receive on your behalf so that the content becomes immediately available to you wherever you are in the world. The second service they provide is to deposit checks they receive on your behalf into your bank account. The third service they provide, for an additional fee, is to mail any packages or credit cards that they receive on your behalf to your address in Country X.

You can then organize the mail that you receive on their servers. Also, you may be able to access mail stored on their servers for years to come, making it easy to look up some information that you received years ago. Traveling Mailbox: www.travelingmailbox.com

---

A possible strategy to avoid state income tax liability is to establish residency in a state with no income tax in a **two-step process**.

The first step: Set up a virtual address in Alaska, Florida, Nevada, New Hampshire, South Dakota, Tennessee, Texas, Washington State and Wyoming. Why one of those states? Those are states that have no state income tax for residents.

The second step: Demonstrate a "nexus" or web of connections tying you to this new state. Let me describe some of the steps you may need to take:

• Once you have a new address, you might consider obtaining, to continue our example in the State of South Dakota, a South Dakota driver's license on the basis of your street address.

• If you have a car that you want to keep, you may consider registering it at the same time that you get a driver's license.

• You may consider registering to vote in South Dakota.

• You may consider changing your address on your banking and investment institutions, and you update your address with Medicare and the Social Security Administration.

• You may consider using a South Dakota CPA to do your taxes.

• You might even consider being seen by a doctor in South Dakota just once. Now you can show proof of all those things to your old state's tax agency (which collects state income tax revenue from that state's residents) when it claims you need to pay taxes there.

Assuming success, once you have been deemed by your former state to be domiciled in Washington State or Nevada or South Dakota or any other state with no income tax, you may have been able to convince the state in which you previously paid state income taxes that you no longer have any state income tax liability in connection with it.

We recommend that you discuss this issue with a U.S. tax lawyer and C.P.A. before attempting anything like this.

Again, we were only using South Dakota as an example. Any state with no state income tax could be used as an adoptive state while you are living in Country X.

IMPORTANT SIDE NOTE

If you have a virtual address in a state with no state income taxes, but you have historically paid taxes to another state, the state in which you formerly paid taxes might continue to view you as a taxable resident until you can convince them otherwise.

YOUR OBLIGATION TO PAY FEDERAL TAXES: Even if you are successful at uncoupling yourself from a state that has state income tax, you may still be obligated to pay federal taxes.

The only exception to your obligation to pay federal taxes would be if your tax and legal team tells you that you are not deemed to be a taxpayer of the U.S., or that you qualify for some kind of tax exclusion or tax credit which would free you from U.S. tax obligations, in which case you may still be required to file a federal U.S. tax return for informational purposes, even if no tax is due.

Here is a list of all of the current U.S. states that do not have any income tax: Alaska, Florida, Nevada, New Hampshire, South Dakota, Tennessee, Texas, Washington and Wyoming.

☆ ☆ ☆ ☆ ☆

For more resources and additional information to help you start an exciting new chapter in your life, please visit our website at www.AllPointsGuide.com.

15. MISCELLANEOUS

Acronyms and ISO Codes for Currency

BRL = Brazilian real (R$)

CAD = Canadian dollar ($) (sometimes CAN$ or C$)

COP = Colombian Peso ($)

CZK = Czech Republic koruna (Kč)

CRC = Costa Rican Colon (₡)

EUR = Euro (€)

GBP = British pound sterling (£)

HKD = Hong Kong dollar (HK$)

IDR = Indonesian Rupiah (Rp)

MYR = Malaysian Ringgit (RM)

MXN = Mexican peso ($)

THB = Thai baht (฿)

USD = United States dollar ($)

AirBnB

A good approach for booking your lodging on AirBnB is to search for a stay lasting 29 consecutive days or longer. This will unlock any monthly discounted rates that may be attached to a given listing. Note that not all AirBnB lodgings give a discount for extended stays.

Further savings might be available for stays lasting months or a year or longer by simply contacting the host and inquiring whether they might consider renting the property to you at a discounted rate.

Affordable Care Act Obligations (U.S.)

Previously, there was a requirement for U.S. taxpayers to have private healthcare in America, either through your employer or through the Affordable Care Act (Obamacare). U.S. citizens that were residents of a foreign country or that lived a requisite amount of time each year in a foreign country were exempt from this requirement.

As of this writing, however, the only obligations to have health insurance are those that are mandated by California, DC and Maryland.

To explore if living in Country X or being a resident of Country X exempts you from those obligations, the following web page provides links to help you explore any possible exemptions that might exist in those three states: https://www.healthcare.gov/exemptions/.

Apps to Have on Your Phone

- Amazon Shopping (same app is used for multiple countries)
- DiDi (get a ride)
- Duolingo (work on your foreign languages)
- Google Maps (share your GPS location in real time)
- Google Translate (translate between languages)
- Kindle (carry helpful books like this around on your phone)
- Maps.me (download maps in case you lose your cell connection)
- Moovit (real time info on public transportation)
- Rome2Rio (global guide for getting from Point A to Point B)
- TripAdvisor (find out where to go, what to do and where to eat)
- TripIt (create and share travel plans with friends and family)
- Uber (get a ride)
- Waze (get directions)
- Weather Underground (get weather forecasts)
- WhatsApp (get connected with people and businesses)
- Wise (transfer money to yourself and others)

Carbon Monoxide Poisoning

While this is not a common phenomenon, it is a threat that is easily addressed by taking a portable carbon monoxide detector with you. You can buy one for about $20 from a retailer like Amazon.

Children of U.S. Citizens Born Abroad

If one or more of your children are born in Country X, they may automatically be deemed to be citizens of Country X. Make sure that you obtain a Country X birth certificate for any child born in Country X.

They may also be eligible for dual citizenship if they are recognized by your country of origin as citizens or nationals of your home country.

If you are a U.S. citizen (or non-citizen national) and have a child in Country X, you should report your child's birth at the nearest U.S. embassy or consulate as soon as possible so that a Consular Report of Birth Abroad (CRBA) can be issued as an official record of the child's claim to U.S. citizenship or nationality. You will need to fill out Form DS-2029:

https://eforms.state.gov/Forms/ds2029.PDF

The only tricky part to obtaining a CRBA is that the embassy may require the parent(s) to prove that they are not only citizens of the U.S., but have been physically present in the United States for a minimum of 5 years (that is 5 years in the aggregate so there may be breaks in between during which the parent left the U.S.), depending on a number of factors discussed here: https://www.uscis.gov/policy-manual/volume-12-part-h-chapter-5.

The evidence necessary to prove physical presence may take the form of passports, tax records, including W2 forms, pay statements or other evidence of employment, photos, school transcripts, apartment leases and annual Social Security statements. So, if you are a U.S. citizen planning to have a child in Country X, make sure to save your old passports, W2 forms, etc., and scan them and/or physically bring them with you to Country X.

If you do not have any of the evidence listed above, the consular officer will advise you at the time of your application about any alternative means that may be acceptable for proving your presence in the United States.

In light of the fact that proving your child is a dual citizen may come with some hurdles, you might consider returning to your country of origin for your child's birth. Then, after your child is born, you can obtain a Country X visa for your child that will allow them to enter Country X. NOTE: We are assuming that your child's eligibility for a Country X visa will piggyback on your own Country X visa or citizenship status.

Currency Converter

There is an easy solution for currency conversions that you are probably carrying around on your phone right now. Go to google.com. Enter the price of something in pesos and then type: "mxn to" and then enter the name of the currency (or its three-letter code) you want for the conversion, as follows:

- For US dollars enter "usd"
- For Canadian dollars enter "cad"
- For Euros enter "eur"
- For British pounds enter "gbp"

As an example, if the price of something costs 500 euros (€), and you want the price in dollars, you can simply enter "500 eur to usd" and hit enter. Google will do the conversion using the real-time conversion rate. Knowing the three-letter code will save you lots of time. You can easily do conversions in reverse by typing the price of something in a different currency and then type words: "to eur." For example, "100 usd to eur" will give you the price of a $100 US dollar item in euros.

Note that you do not need to use the three-letter code. You can type out the full name of the currency. Just be sure to include the name of the country if it is a currency name shared by more than one country such as the dollar (which is used in the U.S., Canada, Australia, etc.) and the peso (which is used in Argentina, Chile, Mexico, the Philippines, etc.).

Emergencies

NOTE: The phone numbers and web pages listed below may have changed by the time you are reading this. We therefore recommend that you check the most current numbers and web links at www.AllPointsGuide.com in our resources section.

Prior to entering Country X, we urge you to consider enrolling in a medical and safety evacuation program that will get you back to your home country in the event of a medical or safety emergency. By using a medical and safety evacuation program, you can return to your country of origin where you have healthcare insurance that will cover you.

MedJet is one such program. Alternatively, if you are only staying for a limited time in a country, you might consider purchasing travel insurance (see Chapter 11) that covers emergent care in Country X as well as medical evacuation to the U.S.

Your MedJet coverage can only cover medical emergencies or it can also cover safety emergencies for an additional fee. Safety emergencies can involve terrorism, kidnapping, natural disaster, violent crime and others.

www.medjetassist.com

If you do not purchase medical evacuation insurance but later find that you need a medical evacuation, the U.S. Embassy in Country X might maintain a database on emergency airlift providers as well as other medical resource data such as doctors that speak English:

NOTE: Medical evacuation may only cover flights from Country X to one or two close-in cities in your country of origin.

The U.S. State Department maintains a web page with helpful web pages for U.S. Citizens living abroad. It deals with what needs to be done when a birth, death, marriage, divorce occurs while abroad. It also provides information about federal benefits and obligations while abroad. You can view it here:

https://travel.state.gov/content/travel/en/international-travel/while-abroad.html

Did you know that you can register your trip with the consulate of your country of origin? If you will be traveling in Country X for more than a few days, register your trip with your consulate before your departure so that they can keep you informed and help get you out of the country in case of extreme weather or political conflict.

We urge you to consider paying for travel, international health and/or medical evacuation insurance. Evacuation coverage is an excellent idea always, but it's especially important to consider it if you will be visiting areas that are more rural or far beyond major tourist areas.

The more adventurous your trip, the more important it is to purchase excellent travel/health/medical evacuation coverage. The fact that you're young and healthy does not guarantee anything, especially when you're in a foreign country.

Epi-Pen

Due to some countries' strict regulation of epinephrine, you may not be able to purchase an Epi-Pen in Country X even with a doctor's prescription.

If you think you might require an Epi-Pen while in Country X due to a medical history of life-threatening allergic reactions such as anaphylaxis, we recommend that you travel to Country X with at least two Epi-Pens or an acceptable substitute prescribed by your physician. Make sure that you take a physician's prescription and letter confirming the medical need for those pens.

Exchange Rates

If, when you are paying with a credit card, you are ever asked at a restaurant or anywhere else if you want to pay a bill in local currency vs. any other currency, choose the local Country X currency option.

An easy way to sidestep this dilemma is to always pay cash. That way there are no exchange rates confronting you. Just make sure you have a mix of denominations with you. If you are only carrying large bills, some establishments will not be able to accommodate you.

Another time that exchange rate problems can crop up is when you are at an ATM. You should know that a common trick that banks try to pull is to offer you a service called Dynamic Currency Conversion (DCC). This is a conversion that isn't done at the official exchange rate. If you opt for a DCC, then you would essentially be allowing the ATM to conjure its own unfair exchange rate.

If your ATM ever gives you an option to decline a conversion, hit "DECLINE CONVERSION."

If your assumption is that the bank will opt to conjure up an exchange rate that is in its own favor, then your assumption is correct. Not only is the exchange rate likely to be in the bank's favor, the DCC service often comes with fees that are often not disclosed.

If you see an offer for Dynamic Currency Conversion (DCC) hit the "no" button. This can be tricky if the message is in Spanish and your Spanish language skills are not very strong, so this is another reason to work on your Spanish proficiency.

Note that transfers from any account in the world into Mexico will result in a change of currency into Mexican pesos.

This underscores the need to time transfers into local Country X currency at times when the peso is weaker than usual against the U.S. dollar. See the section on "TIMING YOUR TRANSFERS OF MONEY TO COUNTRY X " in Chapter 9 for more details about how to determine if it's a good time to transfer money into Mexico.

Global Entry

Global Entry is a program of the U.S. Customs and Border Protection service that allows pre-approved, low-risk travelers to receive expedited clearance upon arrival into the United States through automatic kiosks at select airports and via the SENTRI and NEXUS lanes by land and sea. For information on enrollment visit: https://www.cbp.gov/travel/trusted-traveler-programs/global-entry/how-apply.

Identity Theft

As you strive to prevent identity theft, you may consider a credit monitoring service such as Experian's IdentityWorks which offers different service plans ranging from about $10 per month to about $30 per month. Experian's service reports data from all three of the major credit bureaus to you. It also has a family plan that might offer some savings to you.

If you do not need to source new lines of credit and/or do not need to provide access to anyone in the near future, you might seriously consider freezing your credit. This can be done for absolutely no fees at all three major credit bureaus.

Note that there are no fees associated with a freeze, but there may be a fee associated with a lock. And in some cases, if you need to give someone access to your credit, you can temporarily disable the freeze and set it to resume after a certain amount of days with no additional action needed. Not only can you freeze and unfreeze your accounts for free, freezing and unfreezing will have no impact on your credit score whatsoever.

The difference between a freeze (which is free) and a lock (which may have fees associated with it) is that, while both freeze your credit, a lock includes the services provided by Experian IdentityWorks, namely, notifications regarding all three major credit bureaus.

These are the web pages to use in order to freeze your accounts for free with the three major credit bureaus:

https://www.transunion.com/credit-freeze

https://www.experian.com/freeze/center.html

https://www.equifax.com/personal/credit-report-services/credit-freeze/

Knives, Guns, Ammo & Other Prohibited Weapons

Carrying a knife or pocketknife on your person in some countries can be illegal regardless of the length of the blade and can carry a prison sentence. If you are charged with another type of crime, and they find that you are carrying a knife, you might also face added weapons' charges.

Carrying any kind of firearm, or even a single cartridge of ammunition, around in some countries or bringing anything like that into some countries (without the proper permits issued by Country X that might be hard to come by) may be illegal and may result in a prison sentence of a number of years.

NOTE: You may risk going to prison if you are in a car with someone who is carrying illegal ammunition and/or an illegal firearm.

Laundry

You will likely find that, while washing machines are prevalent in Mexico, dryers are not. If you're living in a home that you own, you may want to consider purchasing a dryer. Clothes dryers are available for purchase in Mexico even if they are not prevalent.

Alternatively, you might consider paying for the use of a washer and dryer at your local laundromat or paying for a full wash-and-fold service. The price of a wash-and-fold service will likely seem very affordable.

Meeting Other Expats

It is a good idea to network with other foreigners, expats and nomads by looking for groups in Facebook and other social media sites. They will become valuable resources. For example, if you are looking for a competent, English-speaking dentist, the best way to find that person might be in an expat forum or group.

Metric System

Mexico uses the metric system of weights and measures. By contrast, the United States uses the imperial system so adjusting to the metric system may require overcoming a bit of a learning curve. Canadians tend to use a hybrid system that combine using the metric system for some things and the Imperial system for others.

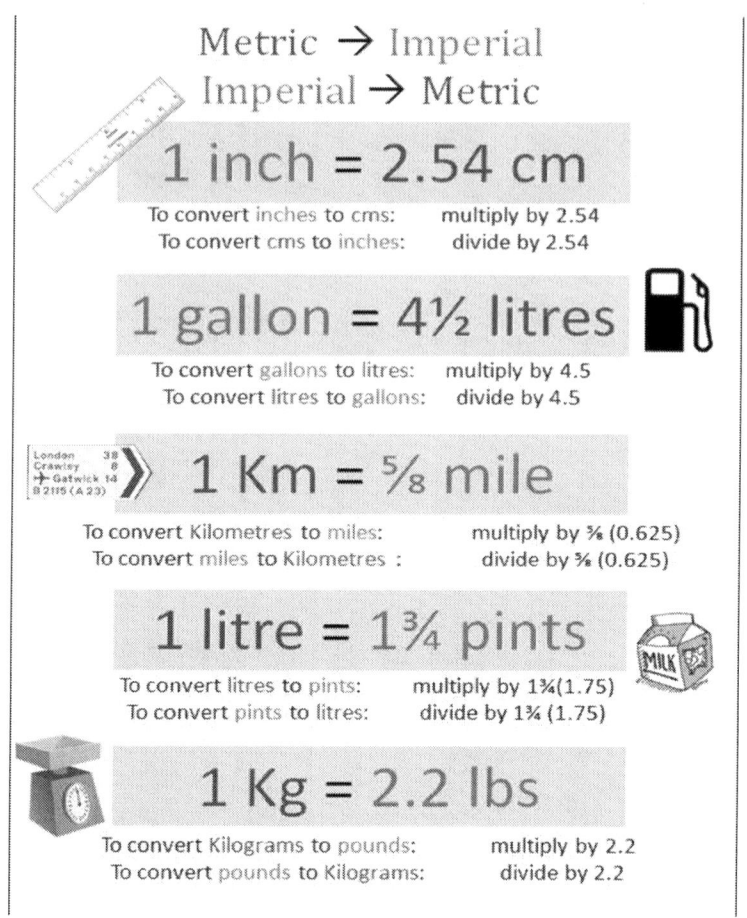

Mobility Issues

Very few countries have benefited from a law (such as the Americans with Disabilities Act in the United States) that requires buildings to provide access to the disabled. Plan for a lack of accommodating features such as ramps.

Even if you do not have a mobility issue, you should watch your step very carefully when walking on streets or sidewalks because they are riddled with holes and other defects. It is very common for pedestrians to sprain, strain, break or tear something in their feet and/or ankles in some countries.

We recommend that you wear comfortable shoes that give you a good grip on the road or sidewalk beneath you. You want soles with lots of traction. You might even consider wearing hiking boots that rise up to support your ankles to prevent a strain or a tear in them.

Movies in Your Preferred Language

Simply google movie theaters where you are living. Look for listings that advertise for showings with the word "SUB." Make sure that you understand the language in which the movie was originally filmed.

Passport Card (U.S.)

The U.S. Passport Card can ONLY be used to enter the United States from Canada, Mexico, the Caribbean, and Bermuda at land border crossings or seaports-of-entry and is more convenient and less expensive than a passport book. The passport card CANNOT be used for international travel by air.

Also, if you are attempting to enter Mexico as a U.S. citizen, Mexico requires that you have a U.S. passport (see below for more information on Passport Requirements).

Our recommendation is that you obtain both a U.S. passport and a U.S. Passport Card. The cost of adding the card when you already have a passport is only $30. If you ever lose your passport, having the card will make it easier to get back into the United States. For best case scenarios, you should never intentionally rely on only a card. Case in point: If you want to obtain a temporary residence visa or a permanent residency visa, you will need to show your current U.S. passport at your interview. A card will not suffice.

Power Outages and Medical Equipment

Power outages are much more common in some countries than they are in the United States. If you rely on any electrically powered medical device such as a respirator or a CPAP machine, then you may want to consider purchasing a back-up battery to keep your medical device functioning in the event of an outage. These are referred to as "uninterrupted power supplies." Here is a URL which lists some possible options: https://www.lifewire.com/best-uninterrupted-power-supplies-4142625.

"Proof of Life"

If you are both (1) living outside of the United States and (2) receiving Social Security benefits from the United States of America you must certify every two years (or every year if you are age 90 or older) that you are still alive using the "proof of life" procedure contained in SSA Form 7162.

The Social Security Administration sends out about 260,000 "proof of life" questionnaires every year. If your social security number ends with any number between 00 and 49, you will receive a questionnaire in even-numbered years. If your social security number ends with any number between 50 and 99, you will receive a question in odd-numbered years.

Note that the mailing of questionnaires may be suspended from time-to-time due to Covid. Also, mail service either in the United States or Country X may not be 100% adequate to get your mail back to the SSA. We recommend that you contact the federal benefits unit at the

U.S. consulate nearest you to find out if you need to fill out an SSA Form 7162. If you do, ask what they suggest guarantees the best way to insure the delivery of your form.

Reverse Osmosis

Note that boiling water may not address all the dangers hiding in the water supply of Country X, especially dangers like arsenic and dangerously high levels of fluoride (a little fluoride is safe). For this reason, you might consider using a reverse osmosis system in your home. This method removes a high percentage of contaminants from water, including heavy metals, nitrates, sulfates, and many more.

Schools

You may decide that the public education system in Country X is not quite as good as the public education system in the U.S. In light of this possibility, coupled with the fact that many parents want their children to learn English, enrolling your children in private and/or international schools may be a good option.

Shopping

If a seller does not ship to Country X directly, however, you would need to have your order shipped to your U.S. mail forwarding service (a service such as flycrates.com and myus.com) and then have them ship the item to you in Country X.

NOTE: Any time the copy states that an item is restricted from delivery to Country X, it should not be purchased by you and sent to your mail forwarder to be sent to you in Country X. That would be a breach of terms and could get everyone in trouble.

Signs in Public: Getting Help with Translations

If you need help translating or understanding a sign you see in public, you may be able to get help by first downloading the app known as Google Lens to your phone, and then following these steps:

1. Go to the Home screen. To open the menu, swipe up on the screen
2. Scroll down. Choose 'Camera'
3. Choose 'More'
4. Choose 'Lens'
5. If you are asked to turn on the camera, choose 'Turn on camera to use Lens'
6. Choose 'Allow'
7. Point the camera at the text you want to translate
8. Choose the translation symbol
9. Optional: Choose English or choose a different language

Smart Traveler Enrollment Program (STEP) (United States)

The U.S. State Department created STEP to send you email alerts about what is going on at U.S. embassies and consulates including travel advisories at https://step.state.gov/step/.

Social Security Benefits (United States)

In order to be eligible to receive Social Security benefits from the Social Security Administration you must have accrued a minimum of 40 credits. If you intend to benefit from the Social Security system (including, possibly, Social Security Disability Insurance, you may need to pay into the system for additional periods of time.

Since 1978, everyone can only earn up to a maximum of four credits per year. Thus, you will need to work a minimum of 10 years (although not necessarily in a row) to reach 40 credits.

Credits are based on your total wages and self-employment income for the year. You might work a full year to earn four credits, or you might earn enough for all four in much less time.

The amount of earnings it takes to earn a credit may change each year. In 2022, you earn one Social Security or Medicare credit for every $1,510 USD in covered earnings each year. You must earn at least $6,040 USD to get the maximum of four credits for the year.

During your lifetime, you might earn more credits than the minimum number you need to be eligible for benefits. These extra credits do not increase your benefit amount.

Rather, it is the average of your earnings over your working years, not the total number of credits you earn, that determines how much your monthly payment will be when you receive benefits.

To check the number of quarters you have accrued as of today, you may be able to check your Social Security statement at https://www.ssa.gov/myaccount/statement.html.

Social Security Card (United States)

If you don't have one, it is a really good idea to obtain a physical social security card (or whatever the equivalent card might be in your country of origin) before you leave the United States. Once you are given a social security card by the Social Security Administration, scan it and save the PDF document in multiple places. You may be asked for copies in the future or you may be asked to produce the actual, physical card itself. This way you will be ready for every eventuality.

Streaming Apps

You may find that streaming apps will play a vital role in your entertainment when living in Country X, and help you stay connected to the culture, news, events, entertainment and sports of your country of origin. Once you get your VPN working, you should be able to watch the same streaming apps that you did in your country of origin. If you are not using a smart TV, you may need to use a Roku or similar piece of hardware to get the following apps from the Internet to your TV:

Best Pay Apps:

Netflix, Disney Plus, HBO Max, Hulu, Apple TV Plus, Paramount Plus, Discovery Plus, Amazon Prime Video, Showtime, Starz, YouTube (has some free content also) and ESPN+ (for watching sports)

Best Free Apps:

Peacock, Pluto TV, Roku Channel, Freevee, Tubi, Crackle, Vudu, Sling Free

Best live TV streaming services:

Hulu + Live TV, YouTube TV, Sling TV, FuboTV, Philo TV, and DirecTV Stream

Timeshares

Purchasing a timeshare does not make a lot of sense in a number of ways, but we will just mention these primary issues:

• The price for the timeshare charged by the management company may not reflect the true economic value of the timeshare. Timeshares are often worth a mere fraction of the price being offered in a sales pitch meeting. To get a better sense of what the value of a timeshare at a particular property is, check what timeshares at that property are selling for in an aftermarket site like ebay or TimesharesOnly here: https://www.timesharesonly.com/.

• Trading the annual use of your timeshare in Mexico with a place in, say, Hawaii may not be as easy as you are told it will be. Thus, you may be stuck having the same vacation at the same location year after year even though you might prefer to experience a variety of destinations.

• The fees, charges and interest rates that accompany your purchase on an annual basis may turn out to be exorbitant.

• The management company that is in place when you purchase the timeshare may disappear in the future.

• A timeshare is unlikely to appreciate or generate income so use caution when you are presented with this option.

Time Zones

Time zones are an important consideration in determining where to live. For instance, how will your new time zone at your new home affect your ability to do business, connect with loved ones, etc.? If you are from the United States, living in Canada, the Caribbean or a Latin American country may keep you in a time zone similar to the one you left behind, if not the same exact time zone. In contrast, if you move to, say, Asia, it might be very difficult to maintain communications with people back home due to living in such a disparate time zone. So, do keep time zones in mind.

Transferring Money to Residents of Country X

Venmo might be a great way to transfer money, but it may not operate in Country X. Look into Wise: https://wise.com/money-transfer-app. You can also use Wise to send money to yourself.

U.S. Consular Services for U.S. Citizens

If you are a U.S. citizen, you may be able to obtain certain services at the U.S. consulate near you. One of these is emergency services, and that was discussed above. Other services may include the following:

• Notary services for documents to be used in the U.S., assistance for when U.S. citizens die abroad (providing a certificate of death that is legal in the U.S. among other things)

• Insurance of or renewal of U.S. passports while abroad, arranging for in-person visits of local jails or prisons for U.S. persons imprisoned abroad

• Assistance in the event of international parental child abduction (if your ex-significant other has illegally taken your child to Country X, for instance)

• Helping to arrange emergency financial assistance, identify local medical and legal assistance for U.S. citizens abroad

Destitute U.S. Citizens living abroad and in need of help overseas should contact the nearest U.S. embassy or consulate or the U.S. Department of State, Office of Overseas Citizens Services, at (888) 407-4747 (or from overseas +1 202-501-4444) and ask for assistance.

U.S. State Department Web Page for U.S. Citizens Abroad

The U.S. State Department maintains a web page with helpful web pages for U.S. Citizens living in other countries. It deals with what needs to be done when a birth, marriage, divorce or death occurs while abroad. It also provides information about federal benefits and obligations while abroad.

https://travel.state.gov/content/travel/en/international-travel/while-abroad.html

Vaccinations

Make sure you are up to date on your routine immunizations. Hepatitis A is endemic to many countries, and you should receive at least the first dose of the hepatitis A vaccine series before travel. Hepatitis B vaccine and even a Typhoid vaccine may also be recommended. The CDC probably has specific advice for you based on your expected destinations: https://wwwnc.cdc.gov/travel/destinations/list.

Water Scarcity

If there are drought or water scarcity issues in the area in which you want to live now or in the future, find out if there are any homes that are capable of meeting their own water needs, such as a home with a private well (see "Well Water" below for some important information about well water safety). If you are looking to live in an area where there is water scarcity and no solutions (such as a desalination plant) on the horizon, it might make more sense to rent a home rather than to buy a home.

WhatsApp

WhatsApp is a messaging service that is tied to your phone number. It is used extensively throughout many countries by both individuals and businesses. Once you have the app set up on your phone, there is a way to put it onto your computer which will enable you to correspond by typing on your computer's keyboard, allowing you a much faster speed. Check our site for information about how to do this.

If you are interested in learning more about how to start an exciting new chapter of your life, you can visit our website at www.AllPointsGuide.com for additional resources.

16. INDEX

OTHER BOOKS FROM ALL POINTS GUIDE

ALL POINTS GUIDE LIVING IN MEXICO by Jason S. Guetzkow, Esq., available in paperback and eBook. This the most accurate, comprehensive and detailed book ever written on the subject of coming from another country to live in Mexico.

ALL POINTS GUIDE WATER & PLUMBING IN MEXICO by Jason S. Guetzkow, Esq., available in paperback and eBook. This book provides a detailed analysis of water and plumbing issues that homeowners and renters might face in Mexico.

Made in United States
Troutdale, OR
11/15/2024

24877107R00111